MAJORING IN PSYCH?

Career Options for Psychology Undergraduates

Fourth Edition

Betsy Levonian Morgan
University of Wisconsin–La Crosse

Ann J. Korschgen
University of Missouri

PEARSON

Boston   New York   San Francisco
Mexico City   Montreal   Toronto   London   Madrid   Munich   Paris
Hong Kong   Singapore   Tokyo   Cape Town   Sydney

Dedication

This book is dedicated to our students.

BLM & AJK

Acknowledgments

This book reflects the ideas and concerns of many psychology undergraduates. We thank them for their honesty and their desire to craft successful careers.

We are indebted to the reviewers who helped shape the content and form of this book: Virginia Binder, California State University at Long Beach; Sung Hee Kim, University of Kentucky; Michael Zeller, Minnesota State University at Mankato, Lorry Cology, Owens Community College; Don Patterson, Jacksonville State University; Harold Siegel, Rutgers the State University of New Jersey; and, Meg Warazynski, University of Wisconsin, Whitewater.

Several people at the University of Wisconsin–La Crosse commented on early drafts of the book and we sincerely appreciate their help: Sue Grams, Lora Schweiso, Carmen Van Voorhis and Teresa Znidarsich. Tim Tritch and Karolyn Bald from UW–L's Career Services have provided excellent information for several editions of this book.

We would also like to thank the people at ACT, especially Patricia Farrant, who allowed us to use some of their "Discover" material and encouraged the production of a book like this. Finally, we would like to thank Allyn and Bacon for supporting the development of this project.

Our special thanks to Adam, Carl, Peter, & Zachary!

Contents

Expanded Contents (Selected Subtopics)

Chapter 10   I have my job, now what?

- ❖ What should my first objectives be in my new job?
- ❖ How do I become effective in my specific work assignments?
- ❖ How do I know if I am "on track" with the direction of my career?
- ❖ How do I keep from making my work my life?
- ❖ What should I do to allow for job change opportunities?

INTRODUCTION

Spending some time and energy thinking about what you want to do, and how to do it, early in your college career can have enormous payoff once you graduate. This guide is intended to help you lay out some of the questions and answers involved in planning a career with a psychology degree. It is designed to be a quick and easy guide to the process—not an encyclopedia. To facilitate your reading of the text, we chose to create a section called "sources" at the end of the book instead of using traditional American Psychological Association (APA) citation format within the text. The information we provide that is based on empirical sources is as current as possible (most have been published since 2004). Finally, we provide references to particularly important resources for almost every chapter. We hope you use them.

Although this book was designed specifically with psychology majors in mind—almost all of it is applicable to other social science majors and to interdisciplinary social science degrees. This is the book we both wish we had read when we were in college. It is a book for the majority of you who will NOT go to graduate school and who will be people who will define the answer to "what can you do with a psychology degree?" for the next several years.

You may skip around in this book, but you may want to read it straight through. Whatever your approach—just think of that nice feeling of satisfaction you'll get having spent some time thinking about your future. Let's get to it!

Feel free to send your comments on this book to either one of us. We'd like to hear from you.

Betsy Levonian Morgan, PhD
Professor
Psychology Department
University of Wisconsin
La Crosse, WI 54601
morgan.bets@uwlax.edu

Ann Jeanette Korschgen, PhD
Vice Provost of Enrollment
Management
University of Missouri
Columbia, MO 65211
KorschgenA@missouri.edu

1

Should I major in psychology?

No one can answer this question for you--except you. Psychology is a fascinating science, and it gives you a solid undergraduate training that is a benefit to many career paths. However, students who are the most successful and happiest with their psychology degrees are the ones who put the extra effort in to making the degree what they want it to be. We have designed this book to be a practical guide to finding and securing a career path where you will best display your interests and talents. So, while we may not know if you should be a psychology major, we can tell you what kinds of questions you should be asking in order to answer that question.

What does it mean to major in psychology? Many students think that they will <u>be</u> psychologists when they graduate with an undergraduate degree in psychology. Unfortunately, that is a false notion. You must have an advanced degree to be a psychologist. However, you will be able to work in psychology-related areas with a psychology BA or BS. More importantly, psychology is a good background for many other fields. Employers are looking for students with good problem-solving skills who can write and speak well. Psychology should provide excellent training in those areas because it is a good all-purpose liberal arts major. Many students go into psychology because they "want to help people." Great! However, there are many ways to help people and many jobs that involve people skills. You need not necessarily get a psychology-related job in order to use the skills you will acquire. In fact, psychology majors are slightly less likely than other majors to work in a job that is directly related to their training (nationally, around 50% say their jobs are closely related to their psychology degree). In this book, we hope to expand your ideas about what kinds of careers are possible with a psychology degree (Chapter 3) and we focus on ways for you to enhance your "marketability" (Chapter 5).

> Psychologists are *obsessed* with rats and dreams... If you like rats or dreams, and above all, if you dream about rats, you should major in psychology. - Dave Barry

Does this quote hit home? While the quote is amusing--it is also nonsense. People unfamiliar with psychology (e.g., those people who turned purple when you told them you were thinking of becoming a psychology major) tend to have a very narrow view of psychology. Your parents, partners, and friends, or anyone who asks the question, "Psychology... what are you going to do with that?!" should be told that psychology provides students with a degree that is a good springboard to a wide variety of choices.
You may also need to expand your vision of what psychology is. Many of us think immediately of the

physician Sigmund Freud and his legendary black couch, or fictional therapists such as Dr. Bob Hartley, Dr. Jason Seaver, Dr. Marlena Brady, or the brothers Frasier and Niles on TV. We tend to assume that all psychologists are therapists or counselors.

Currently, about half of the doctorate degrees in psychology are in the clinical and/or counseling area, but the rest span a wide variety of fields (e.g., developmental, industrial or organizational, social, educational, experimental, neuroscience, etc.). Most of the programs in these areas are extremely competitive and graduate training is expensive. We don't want to frighten you off, but we want you to be sure that you've amply explored what your options are with an undergraduate degree in psychology before you get your heart set on being a therapist. We also don't want you to overlook the two-year master's programs in applied areas that may be a good choice (e.g., school psychology, industrial or organizational, guidance counseling, social work, etc.).

Psst . . . If you find it frustrating that you won't have any specific training when you finish with your bachelor's degree, we suggest that you think about a different major in which you can develop career-specific sets of skills (e.g., accountancy, occupational therapy, nursing, and engineering).

What is the benefit of psychology versus any other degree? Good question. Many students major in psychology because they just find it so darned interesting. We did. But the truth is that a degree in psychology is what you make of it. You will hear this many times in this book, but your best career strategy is to develop a set of skills and interests and then be able to market yourself. What makes you employable will be your particular combination of personal and academic skills. Consequently, throughout this book, we put a lot of emphasis on internships and other professional experiences that help you hone your interests and skills. You will have to play an active role in order to parlay your ability, experience and skills into the type of career you want.

So, what is psychology? We don't mean to imply that psychology is not a unique discipline. Indeed, psychology is both a distinct and diverse field. Its focus on the individual as the unit of analysis is one of its key features. Additionally, psychology is a social science and therefore should provide you with a good understanding of the benefits of the scientific method. Before we highlight a few of psychology's other distinctive features, we'd like to review the concept of a good liberal education. Many people mistakenly think of politics when they hear the terms liberal arts or liberal education. In fact, the "liberal" behind liberal arts refers to freedom of thought. Cronon (1999) writes that a liberal education "aspires to nurture the growth of human talent in the service of human freedom." Cronon also outlines ten qualities of liberally educated persons that we feel are well worth repeating.

1. They listen and they hear.
2. They read and they understand.
3. They can talk with anyone.
4. They can write clearly and persuasively and movingly.
5. They can solve a wide variety of puzzles and problems.
6. They respect rigor not so much for its own sake but as a way of seeking truth.
7. They practice humility, tolerance, and self-criticism.

8. They understand how to get things done in the world.
9. They nurture and empower the people around them.
10. They have the ability to see connections.

We would like to think that a well-intentioned student pursuing his/her education at a well-intentioned institution of higher learning will be liberally educated. However, in a practical way, these skills will serve you well throughout your life, and we will return to skills such as these when we discuss employability in Chapter 5.

In terms of the development of skills, psychology as a discipline is like other liberal arts fields; however, many scholars argue that psychology is special in the "sheer number" of skills and range of knowledge it offers. Hayes (1996) suggests that psychology offers students a wide range of practical and professional skills in addition to a solid liberal education. She highlights a list of skills that mirrors much to the material above but adds the practical and professional skills: literacy, numeracy, computer literacy, information-finding skills, research skills, measurement skills, contextual awareness, interpersonal awareness, problem-solving skills, critical evaluation, perspectives, higher order analysis and practical skills.

In short, it is the focus on research methodology and psychology as a social science that will enhance your repertoire of potential skills. Many general psychology texts start with a definition of psychology like Myers' that reads "Psychology is the science of behavior and mental processes (2004, p. 8)." Indeed, psychologists at all levels of training tend to be interested in explaining, understanding and predicting how humans (and animals) think, feel and act. Many of us are drawn to psychology out of emotional and intellectual interest in humans and humanity. Consequently, we like to think of the discipline as a great combination of the heart and head.

So, no matter what career you pursue, you will be expected to be able to analyze situations and make intelligent choices; courses in psychology should help you develop good critical thinking skills to aid in informed decision making.

So, why should I be a psychology major? There are several reasons to major in psychology. Psychology might be a good major if you:

- Want to signal employers that you have an interest in people and interpersonal skills.
- Want to work in human services.
- Want to continue on in a psychology-related graduate program.
- Want to double major with another field (e.g., biology) to combine several interests.
- Just find the subject fascinating.
- Are planning a career in a field that requires people skills (such as sales or working with   children).
- Want to develop quantitative skills for use in a variety of social science settings.

And, that's just to name a few! Psychology also makes a good minor because it nicely complements other fields. You will be well suited by psychology as a major if you want a broad, well-rounded degree. Because psychology is a diverse field, it offers many opportunities. <u>But</u>, you must play an active role in defining how it will work toward your own career plans.

Nationally, we know that psychology is one of the most popular majors. Over 75,000 students per year are expected to graduate with degrees in psychology for many years to come. Undergraduate psychology majors in the U.S. tend to be predominately female (~70%) and European-American (~75%). National data suggests that most psychology majors end up working in health related activities, administrative/clerical jobs, and social or professional services. Psychology has seen almost a 50% growth in the last several decades and the growth is expected to continue. Is this a good thing? It is a good thing that people recognize that psychology is an important and interesting field. It <u>may</u> not be a good thing for you personally...as it means there will be many other psychology majors "out there" competing with you for jobs and/or graduate schools.

Most discouraging is the fact that roughly only half of the psychology graduates reported that a four-year degree was required for their current job. This sentiment may reflect the fact that undergraduates (in many fields) tend to have unrealistic expectations about the roles they will play in their first jobs. Entry-level jobs in all fields tend to be related to less job satisfaction. On the positive side, the majority of psychology graduates reported they were in jobs that held career potential and even more reported that their current job built on skills from past jobs. These last findings suggest that these college graduates expected their career prospects to improve.

All of this means that <u>if</u> you choose psychology as a major, you will have to "defend" your choice to many people--including yourself. It is our opinion that your best defense is to be knowledgeable about the field and its applications (see some of our references at the end of this chapter in the "Great Resources!" box for some good reading in the area). The rest of this book should help too.

What if I really want to be a counselor/therapist? You will have to get an advanced degree and get licensed in order to practice as a psychologist. Chapters 7 and 8 deal with graduate school issues. It is possible that you may be able to be involved in some closely supervised counseling-type situations with a BA/BS, but you should be wary of situations that place you in positions of responsibility without the proper training. Additionally, even if you think you are good at "helping," you need to be licensed to do so. Bluntly put, you are not qualified to be a therapist just because you are good at helping your friends with their problems.

Will I be able to get a job with an undergraduate psychology degree? Nationally, the vast majority of psychology majors are employed (less than 5% report being unemployed) and report being satisfied with the length of the time to employment (usually within three months of graduation). You might not be working directly in a psychology-related field, but employers are interested in the skills that psychology majors tend to have. This interest is heightened in times where there is a tight labor market. As one recent human resources publication put it, "Liberal Arts Majors are 'In'." Recent surveys of graduates suggest that their baccalaureate degrees are more important than the specific degree in psychology. Regardless of careers available outside of psychology-related fields, the lists of the top occupations for the 21st century frequently include job titles such as psychologist, counselor, and social worker. Although these occupations require advanced degrees, there is no doubt that there will also be BA/BS jobs in the future related to psychology.

Will I make any money? Here is the bad news. Psychology majors do tend to make less money than many other college graduates. Nationally, average starting salaries for individuals with bachelor's degrees are in the low to mid 30s (that's in the thousands), whereas psychology majors tend to start at salaries in the mid to high 20s. Here is the good news. There are four primary ways to increase your earning potential. First, psychology majors tend to earn less because many of the psychology-related jobs are in the public sector (e.g., working in a group home or for a county's social services department) and/or are support-level entry jobs. These types of jobs tend to pay less. So, one way to increase your earning potential is to consider private sector jobs, particularly jobs in the business world (e.g., sales). Second, individuals with advanced degrees in psychology do tend to earn more than those with baccalaureate degrees, so a master's or doctorate degree may be financially beneficial (but not always--read Chapters 7 & 8!). Third, students with superior academic records tend to begin at higher salaries. Finally, many students end up in lower paying jobs because they are unwilling or unable to be flexible in what kind of job they will take or where the job will be. Geographic flexibility and job type flexibility will enhance your earning potential.

Here is a serious note. Many students tell us that they "don't care about the money." Although we think it is admirable to choose a career out of compassion and/or interest, we think you should care about the money and do whatever is possible to maximize your earning potential within your field of interest. You will find that expenses only increase a few years out of college, especially when people start to have new additions to their lives (e.g., partners, mortgages, children, health care costs, pets, automobiles, insurance, etc.). Additionally, as mentioned earlier, psychology tends to attract a higher proportion of female students than male students. As we hope you are aware, recent female college graduates earned approximately 76 cents to every dollar earned by male graduates (the gap is smaller for psychology majors). A major reason for this difference is choice of major and field of work. Finally, we'd like to remind you that there is ample evidence that a college degree (regardless of gender) is still associated with higher wages and better advancement than high school diplomas.

We want you to make career choices based on accurate information and we want you to be happy with your career and your lifestyle. Chapter 6 is all about earning potential and how to maximize it.

What if I already know what I want to be "when I grow up?" Well, there are some students who know what career they want to pursue and they do just that. Many are clueless--and clueless is just fine too. Indeed, most undergraduates change their majors several times during their college careers. The important point here is that many roads lead to Rome (as the old saying goes). Even if you decide late that "Rome" is where you want to go, or take some detours, the worst that can happen is that you'll have to spend more time in school.

If you are someone who knows what you want to do, then you probably know whether or not an undergraduate degree in psychology will serve that purpose. What you might not know is that many other undergraduate degrees may also serve your purpose. Most employers and graduate schools are looking for ability and promise. Specific courses can always be acquired when needed. Chapter 4 is about exploring careers and Chapter 9 is about conducting a job search. Whether you know what you want to do or not, they should help.

After reading all of this, I <u>still</u> want to be a psych major...now, what do I do? We are so pleased you asked... and that's what the rest of this book is all about. We have designed it so that you should have a firm sense of your options when you are done. Chapter 2 entitled "How can I be sure?" is a great place to start. Additionally, don't forget to read Chapter 10; it focuses on some issues you might not think about much as students such as what to do <u>after</u> you get the job or internship. Happy reading!

Great Resources!

Kuther, T. L. (2006). *The psychology major's handbook* (2nd ed.) Belmont, CA: Wadsworth.

Landrum, R.E., & Davis, S.F. & Landrum, T. (2007). *The psychology major: Career strategies for success* (3rd ed.). Upper Saddle River, NJ: Prentice Hall.

McBurney, D. H. (2002). *How to think like a psychologist* (2nd ed.). Upper Saddle River, NJ: Prentice Hall.

Sternberg, R. J., Dietz-Uhler, B. & Leach, C. (2003). *The psychologist's companion: A guide to scientific writing for students and researchers* (4th ed.). NY: Cambridge University Press.

Also, any good "Introduction to Psychology" textbook.

2

How can I be sure?

Is psychology a good fit for you--or is another major more appropriate for your interests and your future? Now is the time to find out, not only to save you future effort and wasted course credits, but also to help you focus on what is most rewarding for you. Read on, because there are important questions you should be asking yourself. Additionally, there are some interesting steps you can take to help you clarify your choice and then make the most of it! Finally, we've outlined a timeline you can use to make the whole process manageable and fun.

If I am thinking of psychology as a major, what can I do to make certain it is right for me? We'll answer this question by identifying several strategies you can implement to develop greater insight into psychology and whether or not it is an appropriate major for you. The strategies are as follows:

Talk to psychology majors. Find students who are psychology majors on your campus--there should be plenty because as we mentioned in Chapter 1, it is a popular major. Ask them to tell you about some of their psychology classes. What were the topics, what projects were required, what was most interesting, what was least interesting? Ask them about their career plans. As they talk, what is your reaction? How do these classes sound? Also ask the students to identify a couple of approachable psychology instructors with whom you could talk.

Talk with psychology instructors. Drop by during their office hours. Ask them about the major, the courses, the career paths of the students who graduate with a major in the field, the expectations of the faculty, and anything else that concerns you. What are your reactions to what they say?

Take some psychology classes. You should take some courses that give you an understanding of the broad theoretical perspectives within psychology (for example, developmental or social psychology). Deciding on psychology after only taking the introductory general psychology class probably isn't a good idea. The introductory survey is usually such a broad overview of the field that it doesn't provide you the depth to make an appropriate decision about the discipline. You should also consider taking courses that reflect the needs of special populations, such as abnormal psychology or multicultural psychology. Finally, most psychology programs will require you to complete courses in statistics and research design. Don't forget that other disciplines such as communications, sociology, and criminal justice may have courses that will help you decide if a psychology-related field is for you.

Go to the career services office early in your academic career. Ask to speak with an advisor who knows about psychology majors. Find out about the typical concerns and opportunities that psychology majors have regarding jobs, internships, and graduate study. Learn about other majors that might also be related to your interests.

Talk with professionals working in the field. You may want to ask the Career Services staff members for names of professionals working in a field that interests you and then contact them to talk about their work.

What do I gain from following the suggestions you just listed? First, you gain a knowledge base about psychology with which you can make a more informed decision. Second, you give yourself an opportunity to react to various sources of information about the field ensuring that you have a broad perspective with which to make a better decision. Finally, by pursuing several of these options, you immerse yourself in the environment of psychology so that you can react on both an objective as well as a subjective level to the field and its possibilities.

What issues or questions should I be considering? Sometimes a career solution that seems logical and appropriate is still not right because it may not match your values or your ultimate goals. Thus, it is important to think through some of the following issues or questions as they relate to what is important to you and to the kind of person you are and want to become.

What issues or questions should I be considering? Being a psychology major means that the focus of your studies, and probably your subsequent career, will be on people. This has implications that we will explore. Also being a psychology major creates a set of expectations in the minds of many regarding your skills, career options, earnings, and future. It is important to address these expectations as well:

❖ Do I like to work with people?
If your answer is tentative, you must explore why. Obviously not ALL psychology majors will work with people, but usually the expectation is that if you majored in psychology you are interested in people. If you are not interested in people from some perspective, we suggest you think again about why you are majoring in psychology.

❖ What about working with people who have problems?
Often psychology majors go into careers where they are working with populations, such as delinquent youth or people with disabilities, who have special problems. Other times psychology majors are working with "normal people" who have normal problems--but still problems. Your reaction to this is important to gauge. If you know you like to work with people, but not people with problems, take heed. You may want to avoid one of the typical career paths of psychology majors, human services work.

❖ Is a psychology major needed for my goal?
Even if you like to work with people, it doesn't necessarily mean that psychology should be your major. Many other majors, such as business, allied health, and communications involve work with people. To make certain that your goals fit comfortably with your academic major, we suggest you start doing some fact-finding about alternative career paths, using the help of campus career advisors. On the other hand, while it is not always necessary, an undergraduate degree in psychology is a good foundation for graduate work in psychology. So, if you

know you want to get a master's degree in counseling, for example, you will be well served with a psychology undergraduate degree. Note that a psychology undergraduate degree is also good preparation for graduate and professional schoolwork in other disciplines as well!

❖ **What should I make of the fact that psychology graduates, generally speaking, earn less money than do many other majors?**

If making money is one of your primary career goals, then you might want to reexamine psychology as a major. There are no "get rich quick" guarantees that come with this discipline, although some graduates do very well financially. Now is a good time to sort through what you value and why. Oftentimes it is an issue of relative importance. If making money is more important than providing direct service or care to an individual with a problem, then you need to acknowledge that and act on it by either thinking of business career options for psychology majors or by majoring in another discipline. (See Chapter 6 for more on earning potential.)

❖ **My parents or other family members insist that I NOT major in psychology. They say it offers me no future. What should I do?**

The first thing to remember is that it is your life and you who will be responsible for the choices that you make. At the same time, it is important to listen to the concerns of your family and to investigate what they say. Certainly share with them the information you learn about psychology from this book and other sources. Majoring in psychology does offer you a future, but whether or not it is the kind of future you want is for you to decide.

❖ **Even though I have the interest in psychology, how do I know that this interest will last me my whole career?**
It may not. And that is OK. Many people change careers. However, research has shown that if your personality matches your work environment, you will be more likely to experience a stable and satisfying career. For example, people who have a social personality tend to do best in an environment that involves interpersonal interactions. To decide if a psychology-related career is a good long-term match for you, in addition to taking the steps we have outlined in this book, you might also want to investigate personality assessment instruments and computerized career advising software, usually offered through career services or counseling and testing offices. These instruments can sometimes reaffirm your choices or help broaden your knowledge of other appropriate options.

OK--I am fairly confident that I want to be a psychology major, what's next? Get involved in your field. And it's not that hard, either. Ask other psychology majors about clubs or organizations. Usually there is a psychology club on campus that brings in interesting guest speakers. Join it. There may be other clubs on campus that you might want to investigate and join. For example, if you are interested in human resources or business or communications, there will probably be organizations on campus that reflect those interests as well. Find out about any volunteer projects that psychology majors are sponsoring --help out. Talk with psychology faculty about research projects with which they might need help. And, importantly, find out about internships and then try to have at least one internship experience before you graduate.

Throughout this book, we talk a lot about the importance of getting field or practical experience (such as an internship) as a way to gain skills, make professional contacts, and find out what you like and don't like to do. In the graduate school chapters we stress the importance of research experience as necessary for graduate school preparation. We want to take some time here to stress the importance of research experience even if you do <u>not</u> go to graduate school! Research experience is excellent training in logical and critical thought. As an employee you might be called upon to weigh research as it pertains to your job. Finally, you will be a consumer of research throughout your lifetime just because you will be trying to assess the pros and cons of various positions. We have used our research training in such various situations as choosing among medical care options, deciding on our children's schooling, making career changes, and planning our financial futures. We use it often when we read the paper or a popular magazine, and you will too. It is a useful skill.

What else might help me now as I plan my psychology major? Plan your coursework. If there are courses you want to take to complement your psychology major, such as courses in criminology, human resources, marketing, or writing, it is essential that you think through which courses you want, when you want to take them, and what prerequisites they might have. Otherwise you can end up graduating without some of the academic breadth you need to enhance your marketability.

How can I do ALL that you are suggesting? There's an easy answer to that. Develop a timeline, which is a detailed plan designed to help you work through your academic and career interests in a systematic and savvy way. It is like a road map to help you navigate your academic career with the best possible outcomes in mind. Here is a suggested timeline; however, it may need to be adjusted according to your own personal needs and academic schedule, especially if you are a part-time student.

TIMELINE

FIRST OR SECOND YEAR:

- ❑ *Decide on whether or not to major in psychology. Visit with instructors, talk with career services advisors, and seek advice of current psychology majors, alumni, and employers. Sit in on classes, read about career options, learn about possible internships (see Chapter 5 for more information on internships), and talk with friends and family.*

- ❑ *If you are majoring in psychology, then discuss your specific interests with a career advisor. How might you use your interest in psychology in a work setting? See Chapter 3 for examples of some of the jobs available to a psychology major. Explore these options and think through the implications of the choices they offer. For example, your interests will dictate the type of courses you will want to take, the type of internship(s) that you will want to have,* and even the campus clubs and organizations that you will want to join.

❑ **Identify the courses that you will want to take to complete your major as well as other courses or a minor that will complement your interests.** *See what prerequisites exist, when the courses are offered, what special approvals you may need to take the classes, and any other actions that are needed on your part now to ensure you can accomplish what you need to do.*

Psst . . . You will find it beneficial to develop computer skills, in particular, a word processing program, a statistical package, and a spreadsheet.

THIRD YEAR

❑ **Begin to build your resume.** *You will need a resume (a summary of the highlights of your education and work experiences) for applying for an internship. In addition, if you begin to build your resume early in your academic career, you will be better able to remember the significant aspects of your education and your work experiences that will be important for a future employer to know.*

❑ **Examine internship options and discuss them with an internship coordinator.** *Determine if any requirements exist, such as grade point average or year in college that would affect your application plans. Also identify what special documentation is needed for applying, such as special application forms or a resume.*

❑ ***Get involved in campus organizations, volunteer projects, or a research project.*** *Join psychology clubs, become an APA student affiliate, or join any other organizations that will enable you to learn about your profession as well as to make a contribution of your time and talent. Also, this is a good time to work with an instructor on a research project.*

❑ ***Consider graduate school options.*** *See Chapter 8 for a suggested timetable to use to examine graduate school possibilities.*

❑ ***What else?*** *Use the resources on campus! Go to career days, browse through the materials in the career library, talk to faculty, search the Internet--all to learn as much as you can about psychology, your options within it, and how to best use your skills.*

FOURTH YEAR

❑ ***Begin your job search.*** *Use the career services' employer referral services, participate in on-campus interviews, access vacancy listings, and read Chapter 9 (How do I do a job search?).*

❑ ***If you are considering graduate school, see Chapter 8 for steps to take.***

❑ ***Continue with the activities*** *we outlined for your junior year, such as being involved in campus organizations, continuing to build your resume, and assisting in a research project with an instructor.*

What if I have declared a psychology major late in my academic career--what good is a timeline? You may need to accelerate some of the steps we have outlined in the timeline, but even so, they will be useful to you no matter when you declare psychology as your major. We especially encourage you to get to know your instructors and to have an internship experience.

What do I do if I decide that psychology is NOT the best major for me? Our motto is "It's never too late to make a change." One option would be to switch completely to another major but that may cost you in time and money. Another option would be to finish the psychology major but pick up additional courses in an area of interest. Or you might do internships in your area of interest. We suggest you talk with an academic and a career advisor regarding the best strategy for you.

What if I am more and more sure about psychology and less and less sure about career options that are available? We know this is a big issue. Will you get a job? How much money will you make? What kinds of jobs are available? Read on, as we will address these important topics in the next chapters.

Great Resources!

Borchard, D. C., Bonner, C., & Musich, S. (2002). *Your career planner* (8th ed.). Dubuque, Iowa: Kendal/Hunt.

Corey, G. & Corey, M. S. (2006). *I never knew I had a choice*: *Explorations in personal growth* (8th ed.). Belmont, CA: Thompson/Brooks/Cole.

3

What careers are available for psychology majors?

You may have the mistaken idea that there are "no jobs" out there for psychology majors. In fact, psychology majors are highly employable. Many psychology students work in areas that you might not originally think of as "psychology-related." Consequently, you will be well served by expanding your ideas about what constitute "careers with a psychology degree" and by learning how to successfully market your abilities and interests to a wide variety of employers. In this chapter we will discuss careers that are well suited for psychology majors, we will provide a chart of major categories of jobs in which psychology students tend to be employed, and we will take an in-depth look at three jobs in terms of their responsibilities, salaries, and expected growth.

What kinds of jobs are "right" for psychology majors? As we have stated earlier, research suggests that employers tend to look for global qualities as well as specific skills. Employers say that they look for good communication skills (written and verbal), good interpersonal skills, teamwork ability, flexibility, and analytical skills. Additionally, technological skills (such as computer and Internet skills) are a real benefit to any student in any field. Most psychology programs should serve to improve your abilities in each of those areas. So, in many ways, psychology is a good background for many different types of work.

Psychology is also a field particularly well suited to careers that involve "helping people." And, we know that many students choose psychology because they find it interesting and they want to "help people." So, it is no surprise that many psychology majors work directly in fields where they help people one-on-one. For instance, psychology majors work in group homes, hospitals, nursing homes, correctional facilities, juvenile detention facilities, pre-schools, shelters, and local, state and national human services (to name a few).

However, it is also helpful to view your psychology degree more widely and see it as a good general liberal arts degree that sets you up for many potential careers. We do not mean to suggest that you can just graduate with a psychology degree and be offered a job. We do mean to suggest that you can develop a set of skills and interests while in college that are attractive to many employers. The more specific those skills are to a particular field, the more attractive applicant you will be. We know an employer in banking who specifically recruits psychology majors because he believes that they tend to have better interpersonal skills. He says he can train them in the specifics of the job!

We have had more than a few students joke with us about ending up with a career in fast food. These jokes reflect students' genuine worry about their future career prospects. We don't find these jokes particularly funny for several reasons. First, if students fall prey to the cynical view that they will never get a good job, they will be less likely to take the actions necessary to secure good employment with advancement opportunities. Second, many students resort to jobs that they think are beneath them because they are not knowledgeable about their other options. When they graduate, they tend to migrate to jobs that are familiar from their high school and/or college experiences, and such jobs tend to be the type that are less interesting and pay less. Third, fast food managerial positions actually have many attractive advancement opportunities and should not be written off summarily. (This is not a joke; managers' salaries are decent in these fields!)

Finally, we feel that students need to expand what it means to them to "help people." Anyone who has worked in sales knows that a good salesperson helps people! Service jobs are some of the fastest growing jobs in the labor market, and service jobs require good people skills. In a similar vein, don't underestimate the importance of your technological skills. A student with a working knowledge of a statistical program such as SPSS will find that this technological skill alone is a genuine foot-in-the- door for some well-paying jobs in finance, marketing, and research-related jobs.

One of the other issues you may not have thought much about is the difference between "jobs" and "careers". The term career implies the concept of advancement and progression; whereas a "job" tends to reflect any set of responsibilities done to make money. Research suggests that most people are more satisfied with the attributes associated with careers.

Consequently, as you think about your futures, we want you to think about building careers rather than just linking jobs. We are not speaking purely to the idea of promotion and advancement. To us, the concept of building a career entails creating a fit between your talents and interests and the responsibilities of your work so that you can create opportunities for change and growth.

Finally, graduate degrees open another whole set of additional career choices. The chapters on graduate school will help you think about these options, but we direct you to the career publications and the web page of the American Psychological Association.

We are trying to get you to think more broadly about the types of jobs for which psychology might be "right." Additionally, we are trying to get you to clarify for yourself what kinds of employment would be OK. What are the qualities of the job that are important to you? What kind of settings? What kind of pay? All of these sorts of questions directly affect which types of jobs you will find interesting <u>and</u> how you can use your psychology degree to get there. Let's look at some categories of jobs and some individual careers that may be of interest to you.

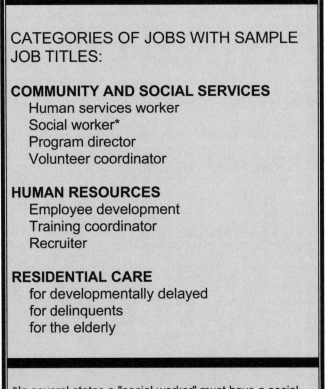

CATEGORIES OF JOBS WITH SAMPLE JOB TITLES:

COMMUNITY AND SOCIAL SERVICES
Human services worker
Social worker*
Program director
Volunteer coordinator

HUMAN RESOURCES
Employee development
Training coordinator
Recruiter

RESIDENTIAL CARE
for developmentally delayed
for delinquents
for the elderly

*In several states a "social worker" must have a social work degree and license, but other states use this title for people with psychology-related backgrounds who work in jobs with social work types of duties.

CATEGORIES OF JOBS
WITH SAMPLE JOB TITLES
CONTINUED:

MANAGEMENT AND BUSINESS
Banking
Sales
Public relations
Restaurant & Hotel
Buyer

STUDENT AFFAIRS/SERVICES
Admissions
Career services
Residential life
Student activities
Alumni/development

PROBATION/PAROLE/LAW ENFORCEMENT
Parole officer
Correction officer
Juvenile intake worker

EDUCATION
Child care worker
Peace Corps
Teacher's aide

SCIENTIFIC RESEARCH
Opinion survey researcher
Marketing researcher
Jury consultancy

As you look at the previous tables, you should realize how varied those categories of work are, and you should think about <u>why</u> some of the jobs appeal to you more than others. If some of the jobs are unknown to you, it is worth looking into them to see if they might be good career options for you. To aid in that direction, we will now take a look at three specific jobs from the tables in order to get a feel for what kinds of tasks and settings are involved. More importantly, by reading these descriptions you will get a sense of what type of information you can access as a student looking into careers. This in-depth information has been adapted from a computerized career advising software called "Discover" developed by American College Testing (ACT), and is being used with ACT's permission. Below we look at the job descriptions for a human services worker, a parole officer, and a human resource recruiter. We chose these three professions because they are directly psychology-related and will give you a sense of the typical work available for psychology majors.

HUMAN SERVICES WORKER

<u>Work tasks</u>. Human services workers tend to work in a variety of settings and are directed by professional staff. They may offer some direct services such as leading groups or offering one-on-one aid. They often help clients with bureaucratic "red tape." If they work as case aides, they may transport clients to various appointments. Often they are involved in helping to determine a client's eligibility for various programs or services. In general, human services workers deal with people one-to-one and with forms and documents appropriate to the setting.

Work settings. There are a wide variety of settings in which human services workers are employed. Here is a list of common sites: groups homes, halfway houses, community mental health centers, hospitals, public welfare agencies, nursing homes, facilities for the developmentally delayed, and private agencies servicing specific populations (for example, autistic people).

Salary potential. The average salary in 2007 was $27,500 for all workers in the field, $32,000 for those with experience. Starting salary average was $22,500; however, this number reflects both employees with and without college degrees so it is undoubtedly higher for students with bachelor's degrees. Advancement usually requires a bachelor's degree or a master's degree in a psychology-related field.

Projected demand for new workers. The projected demand is large. This category of work is expected to grow by rapidly (mostly due to the aging population).

Qualities of the job you may *like*. Human services workers tend to enjoy the satisfaction of helping others and meeting many different people. They also enjoy excellent employment opportunities and working a 40 hour week.

Qualities of the job you may *dislike*. Human services workers tend to find that the work can be emotionally draining and that they are under pressure from under-staffing and lack of resources. They also tend to dislike the fact that it can involve shiftwork and evening and weekend work.

Personal qualities helpful to the job. It is helpful to have:

❖ A strong desire to help others
❖ Patience, understanding and caring in dealing with
   others
❖ Good communication skills
❖ A sense of responsibility
❖ An ability to manage time effectively.

PAROLE OFFICER

Work tasks. Parole officers counsel juvenile or adult
offenders about activities related to their parole (the
conditional release from a correctional facility). They
serve to help clients adjust to life outside prison in the
hope of minimizing the possibility of future criminal
acts. They spend most of their time supervising
offenders by telephone, office visits, and/or home
visits. They also meet with lawyers, law officials, and
the offender's family. They are involved in preparing
reports and testifying in court.

Work settings. Parole officers work for the parole and
probation departments of local, state, and federal
governments. About half their time is in offices,
courtrooms, and prisons; whereas, the other half is
spent traveling in the community to meet clients and
other individuals involved in the situation.

Salary potential. The average salary in 2007 was
$47,000 for all workers in the field. The starting salary
average was $31,500, salaries for experience workers
averaged $58,500. A bachelor's degree is a minimum
requirement. Advancement generally requires a
master's degree and licensing or certification in social
work.

Projected demand for new workers. The projected demand is moderate.

Qualities of the job you may *like*. Parole officers tend to like working with people, helping people solve their problems, the challenge and variety of their work, and knowing about the correctional system.

Qualities of the job you may *dislike*. Parole officers may dislike having to work evenings and weekends, the pressure from under-staffing and heavy workloads, governmental "red tape," working with difficult clients, and becoming emotionally drained in some cases.

Personal qualities helpful to the job. It is helpful to have:
❖ A basic concern for people and their problems
❖ Emotional maturity, objectivity, and sensitivity
❖ An ability to make sound decisions
❖ An ability to be fair and firm
❖ An ability to handle responsibility
❖ An ability to work independently
❖ Knowledge of community agencies/services.

HUMAN RESOURCES RECRUITER

We have chosen to describe the recruiter position because it is typical of an entry level job in human resources. However, a description of a human resources manager is also available.

Work tasks. Human resources seek out, interview, screen and recruit job applicants to fill existing company job openings. They maintain contacts within the community and may travel extensively (often to college campuses). They screen and interview candidates, and conduct background and reference checks.

Work settings. Human resource workers work indoors in offices in virtually every industry: business, health, management, education, labor organizations, manufacturing, finance, insurance, and government.

Salary potential. The average salary in 2007 was $48,000 for all workers in the field, $57,000 for those with experience. The average starting salary was $37,500, and applicants with college degrees are preferred (especially those who have coursework in human resources, personnel, or labor relations). Advancement is usually contingent on ability and experience.

Projected demand for new workers. The projected demand is expected to grow rapidly.

Qualities of the job you may *like*. Human resource workers tend to like their pleasant working conditions and the good salaries and benefits. They also tend to like the ability to travel and being able to interest others in their company's line of work.

Qualities of the job you may *dislike*. Human resource recruiters may tend to dislike the difficulty of finding the right person for the position. In other human resource jobs, workers may dislike informing employees that they have been laid off or fired, and occasionally working long hours to see a project through on deadline.

<u>Personal qualities helpful to the job</u>. It is helpful to have:

❖ Good communication skills
❖ An ability to work as part of a team
❖ Patience, emotional stability, and flexibility
❖ Good computer skills
❖ An ability to function under pressure.

Information on the career guidance software "Discover" is available from ACT at *www.act.org/discover* or (319) 337-1631.

SUMMARY

These three in-depth job descriptions were selected to give you a feeling about several jobs available with a psychology degree that are more typically psychology-related. More importantly, they give you a sense of the type of information you can access about almost any specific career. We have included good resources for you at the end of this chapter, and you will want to read this chapter in conjunction with Chapter 9 on job search strategies.

Great Resources!

American Psychological Association
 (2003). *Psychology scientific
 problem solvers: Careers for the
 twenty-first century.* Washington
 D.C.: Author.

You can download from website in pdf
format from *www.apa.org* or contact APA
at 1-800-374-2721.

DeGalan, J., & Lambert, S. (2006).
 Great jobs for psychology majors.
 (3rd ed.) Lincolnwood, IL: VGM
 Career Horizons.

Kuther, T. L. & Morgan, R. D. (2007).
 *Careers in Psychology:
 Opportunities in a changing world*
 (2nd ed.). Belmont, CA:
 Thompon/Wadsworth.

O'Hara, S. (2005). *What can you do
 with a major in psychology?*
 Hoboken, N.J. Wiley.

4

How do I explore careers?

There are many ways to get quick and accurate information about career options and many ways to explore careers. This chapter will highlight several sources of information including instructors, career services, the library, clubs, alumni and friends, relatives, and practicing professionals. We also have a section on the Internet, which has become a powerful career resource.

Where do I start? As a college student the two best places to start your career exploration are with your instructors and the career center at your institution. Almost every school has some person or people whose work is to assist students with exploring career opportunities. Though they may differ in name, we will refer to this type of place as "career services." Both are excellent places to start! However, there are many other great sources of information including the library, alumni and the Internet. Let's take a look at their offerings...

What do they have to offer?

Instructors. See those old people in the corner
snoozing over their lecture notes? Those are your
faculty. They know something! They can serve as
important resources. Most instructors realize that it is
difficult and frustrating to make career decisions and
they can often be well informed and compassionate;
however, individual instructors vary in how useful they
can be to you. It will be up to you to find faculty who
are both useful and user-friendly. On your part, you
should be clear about <u>what</u> it is you need so that they
can determine their role. For instance, if a student
comes to Betsy (one of the authors of this book) and
says, "I'm totally clueless about what I want to do,"
Betsy will most likely punt to the people on campus
who have more experience discerning students'
interests and aptitudes. Often the career services office
has tests and inventories that are a helpful first step.
However, if a student says, "I know I like psychology ...
but I don't know what kinds of jobs are available" or "I
want to go to graduate school but I'm not sure in what,"
Betsy can help guide the next set of questions which
may help clarify the process. Some faculty don't want
to or cannot answer these questions. Don't get
discouraged--find someone who will. It is our opinion
that the best way to encourage faculty members to be
more receptive to your questions is to do some
legwork beforehand. If you have tried to think through
your concerns enough to ask specific questions, it is a
help.
By the way, thinking through your questions is
beneficial in general (in college and in the real world).
Think about the difference between "I didn't
understand your lecture on Piaget" and "I understood
that Piaget believed that children go through stages of

cognitive development... but you said the structure of the mind changes, and I don't understand how that is related to stages." Whoa... we might appear to be off topic a bit; however, in interviews and in professional situations, it is often helpful for you to provide the context for your questions and concerns.

Psst . . . Faculty do not know everything! They may appear to, but they do not. It is up to you to do a thorough search. Talk to more than one faculty member. Also, remember that most of your faculty members probably did not build a career with a BA/BS in psychology. They probably went to graduate school soon after obtaining a bachelor's degree. So, although they will be a great resource, you should also use other resources to get a full picture of what is available.

Career Services. Most career services offices offer a myriad of resources to help you. Here is a list of the kinds of things your career services office may be likely to offer:

1. Career Exploration: Tests, inventories, and career counseling to help you determine what kinds of careers might be best for you.

2. Resume preparation: You can establish your resume on the web through many career services offices. In that process, the staff will help you review your resume to ensure it best presents your accomplishments. Once it is on the web, you can readily change it as needed and oftentimes it is made available to employers.

3. Arranging internships: Often career services offices are involved in maintaining lists of employers and sites in the area who will take student interns. As we have indicated several places in this book, we think an internship is one of the most important things you can do to enhance your career opportunities.

4. <u>Arranging a job shadow</u>: Frequently, career services offices can arrange for you to accompany a professional throughout a portion of his/her workday. This process of "shadowing" is an excellent way to get a better feel for a job you think might be right for you.

5. <u>Making alumni contacts</u>: Career services offices usually have lists of alumni who are willing to be contacted about career opportunities. Frequently, employers come to trust certain universities and their students so they may be more prone to hire another alum from "Cheesehead U" or wherever. Alumni are also helpful because they may have insights into what you might want to do while you are still in school to enhance your employment possibilities.

6. <u>Job listings and searches</u>: Many career services offices provide lists of jobs that are available (usually by major or area). Others belong to on-line lists or can send your resume out on-line. They can also help you find listings for specific geographic areas.

7. <u>Employer contacts</u>: Career services offices frequently develop relationships with specific employers and know their needs and desires. Oftentimes employers will come to campus to interview or attend career days. This is an excellent (and lower stress) way to explore potential careers.

8. <u>Graduate school preparation</u>: Career services offices usually can help with graduate school preparation, including graduate school and professional fairs, reference guides, and lists of schools. Additionally, they can probably guide you to help for graduate exams (e.g., GREs, LSATs, MCATs, etc.) and they may be willing to read and comment on your personal statements. Remember, it pays to start graduate school preparation early in your college career!

9. <u>Interview practice</u>: No one pops out of their birth mother "good" at being interviewed! It is a skill and, like

all skills, gets better with practice. Many career services offices will run you through mock interviews to better prepare you for the "real" thing.

10. Individualized career help: Many career   services offices will let you schedule or drop by for one-on-one career advising.

Overall, it has been our experience that students have been too reticent to find out what a career services office has to offer. Don't be shy or afraid! March up and say, "I'm trying to decide on a career, can you help me?"or "I'm graduating soon and want to work in Ethiopia... can you help?" Each of the students we know who took the time to learn what their career services had to offer benefited from the experience.

Where else do I look?

The library. Libraries house many useful traditional and electronic resources.

1. Guides: Most libraries have career exploration guides, financial aid guides, and graduate school guides.

2. Individual searches: You can always use the libraries' resources to research specific employers or graduate schools. In other words, it is an excellent place to do your homework on places of interest to you.

Professional clubs or associations. Frequently, departments have major clubs such as the "Psychology Club" or honors clubs such as "Psi Chi" or

"Psi Beta" that sponsor career related events such as alumni panels or guest speakers. In addition, Psi Chi has a good publication called *Eye on Psi Chi* and an extensive website (*www.psichi.org*). Many professional organizations for professionals offer student rates. Especially if you are considering graduate school, you might want to join an organization like the American Psychological Association (APA). Their newsletter, *Monitor on Psychology*, has articles of interest to undergraduates and job listings for people with advanced degrees. It is a good way to get a sense of the field. The Association for Psychological Science (APS) also has a student rate and is a good investment for students interested in research-oriented and/or college teaching careers. We provide the website addresses for both APA and APS later in this chapter.

Alumni. Even if career services doesn't keep a list of alumni, faculty or the alumni office might know some. They are a rich source of knowledge. It is particularly good to hear from those who graduated recently so you can hear about the "current" job market. As always, it is just one person's opinion, so talk to several alums if possible.

Your family and friends. Do not nod off when your Uncle Ernie starts to talk about his buddy's son who works in human resources! Networking is alive and well and a major source of job contacts. Use your personal contacts to initiate professional contacts. It is an excellent way to get a sense of several different types of jobs.

Local professionals. If the career services office doesn't line up job shadowing, then do it yourself. We've had several students call up local professionals and ask to shadow or ask to interview the professional about his/her job. Students are always surprised about how helpful this is.

Psst . . . Not all career exploration leads you to what you want to do. Frequently, it works more like a process of elimination... you find out what you don't want to do. While it might not feel as warm and fuzzy as an "Aha this will be my life!" it is still helpful.

The Internet
The Internet has become a powerful career tool. Below we make a few general statements and give you a few places from which you can take off. However, your career services office can likely provide more help.

Where do I start?
Because the web is not centrally organized you will want to sample a lot of what it has to offer. You will also want to familiarize yourself with search strategies that can save you hours of time. Below we have provided a bunch of great sites that are perfect start-up points for psychology majors. We have also provided some examples of sites where you can do some career exploration.

Some traditional web sites in psychology:
- American Psychological Association (APA): *www.apa.org*
- Association for Psychological Science (APS): *www.psychologicalscience.org*
- Psi Chi--The National Honors Society in Psychology: *www.psichi.org*

Some additional great sites for psych majors (note that most of these sites are put up by caring faculty and they are really helpful places):

- Scott Plous at Wesleyan has a site devoted to general psychology and social psychology—including links to graduate programs. One of the best sites for psychology undergraduates. *www.socialpsychology.org*
- Linda Walsh's site at the University of Northern Iowa
  www.uni.edu/walsh/linda1.html

A sample of some great places to do career searching or exploring on the Web (some may involve fees or subscriptions but you will be warned before you spend any money).

- Hotjobs (*www.hotjobs.com*). Good for entry level job searches – fewer jobs than MonsterTrak (below) but more privacy.
- MonsterTrak (*www.monstertrak.com*). This site is the college graduate portion of Monster.com and is undergoing large changes that might affect its usefulness.
- *Indeed.com* and *SimplyHired.com* are both web-based search engines for jobs and are new editions to the field that have been well received for serving the job hunter.
- The National Assembly of Health and Human Services Organizations (*www.nassembly.org*). Has a link to jobs and internships across the nation.
- Another good tip for work in human services is to visit the local United Way website for the geographical area for which you are interested and find the list of agencies they support and

follow-up to see if any of the agencies have job openings.
- Federal Government Job Listings (*www.usajobs.opm.gov*). America'sJob Bank (*www.jobsearch.org*). This site is no longer maintained but it does provide links to state specific job sites.

Psst . . . If you are looking for a career in human services, many of employers in this area advertise in their local newspapers as they do not have large advertising budgets. Consequently, check to see if the job site you've chosen crawls newspapers for jobs and/or visit the classified ads of the paper in a town in which you'd like to work. *www.careerbuilder.com* searches newspapers as do *www.indeed.com* and *www.simplyhired.com.*

International opportunities?
Both employers and students have shown an increased interest in global opportunities for students. Here are good places to start looking for an internship or work experience abroad. Even if English is the only language in which you are fluent – there are multiple opportunities.

- *http://www.peacecorps.gov* - The Peace Corp is selective and volunteers commit to 27 months of training and service overseas.
- *www.bunac.com* – Bunac offers information an shorter and longer term opportunities involved in working, teaching and/or volunteering abroad for student from U.S.A., Canada, UK and Ireland.
- *http://www.crossculturalsolutions.org* - Cross-Cultural Solutions specializes in international volunteer programs.
- *http://idealist.org* - Idealist focuses on nonprofit information and resources.

- *http://www.jetprogramme.org* - this site focuses on programs associated with teaching English in Japan.
- *http://www.uwlax.edu/careerservices/TIER3/intl/intl _employment.HTM* - this is a site from Career Services at the University of Wisconsin – La Crosse that organizes excellent information about working internationally.

Educational experiences abroad are also excellent opportunities. If your university or college does not have an international education office – seek out one that does – there are semester, annual and summer term options. Another good resource is *http://www.studyabroad.com.*

Keep in mind that web site addresses change fairly often, so don't be surprised if one of the addresses is no longer correct. Finally, please remember that the web is not authoritatively reviewed. Information gained from the web may be unreliable. It will benefit you to check out the sponsor of any web site that you are going to use for academic or personal reasons. However, the web has opened a lot of new possibilities— and you should put it to use for your career preparation.

Why do I need to use all of these resources? When most of us got our first job, we were dropped us off in front of the fast food restaurant or mall entrance and we shuffled in with the application all filled out in our best handwriting. Most college graduates aren't looking for a "job"--they want a career. They are looking for a professional opportunity that provides them advancement possibilities, interesting work, and decent pay. Most careers don't just show up in your life by the way of a "help wanted" poster in a window. Therefore, you must put in the effort to educate yourself about the possibilities. We guarantee (sorry, no money back) that you will be glad you did!

Great Resources!

Check out the web – two of our picks:

Rutger's College Majors and Career Information
http://careerservices.rutgers.edu/ CareerHandouts.html

Quintessential Career's site
http://www.quintcareers.com /choosing_major.html.

5

How do I enhance my employability?

As a psychology major, you <u>will</u> get a job---unless you just do nothing. But there is much you can do <u>now</u> that will enhance your career options. In fact, the actions you take while in college determine the type of job that you will obtain later.

What do I need to be doing now about my future employment? First things first. Employers believe that your past performance predicts your future behavior, and many are making hiring decisions based on that assumption. In fact, to learn about your past behavior, more and more employers are using an interview technique called "behavior-based interviewing" in which they ask you to recall behaviors that you have exhibited in the past. Examples of these behaviors could include how you solved a specific problem working with a group of people; how you provided a service to someone in need; or when you demonstrated leadership in a work situation. Employers are interested in knowing about your "track record" which means that you should be building a history to carry with you into the future. But how?

Building a history is not as hard as you think, especially when you understand what you need to do. And as you start taking the necessary steps, you will discover that enhancing your "marketability" (which means your ability to sell yourself as a candidate to employers) also enhances your academic journey as a student. And hey, why not get two benefits for the price of a single effort?

So why should I care about my "marketability"? It can make a <u>big</u> difference in whether you end up in a job that is a career stepping stone or a career roadblock.
Have you ever seen someone in a job they hated? Or, someone who had stagnated in their work? We have. They have been former students who have come back to us saying they had been too busy as college students to think smart about their own lives. They failed to take some steps in college to ensure they optimized their opportunities. We don't want the same to happen to you and it doesn't have to! You can do things now that will lead you to work that will be meaningful and rewarding for you.

What are some steps to optimize my opportunities? These steps will take some effort, we admit, but the payoff is well worth it. (Take them in the order that makes most sense for you.) We list them below and then we explain each step more fully later in this chapter.

Steps to enhance your employability:
1. **Get to know your faculty.**
2. **Get to know and use resources that can assist you.**
3. **Volunteer some of your time and talent to campus or community organizations.**

4. **Participate in at least one (if not more) internship experience.**
5. **Take coursework that supports your plans.**

1. First of all, what does it mean to "get to know my instructors?" To get to know your instructors, drop by and ask them questions about class or provide them with comments about the class discussions. Talk with them about the field of psychology and their own career paths. Share with them your concerns about your career plans. Ask faculty members to guide you through an independent study or an internship. You might want to assist them with special projects or research. Faculty members have a lot of wisdom to share. They may also have insights that assist you with your choices. Finally, they will be asked to recommend you for work or for graduate study. You want them to know you well and be aware of your skills and abilities so they can speak with enthusiasm about you.

2. What kinds of resources are there and how can they help me? As outlined in Chapter 4 on exploring careers, there are many resources available on campus: faculty, alumni, senior students, the library, and career services.

All of these resources can help you identify your areas of interest and decide upon special courses you could take to help you explore these areas more deeply and to enhance your marketability. They also can often provide you with names of alumni who are willing to talk with you about their careers, information about job opportunities in psychology, leads on job opportunities, and often information on internship options.

3. Why do I need to take time to do volunteer work? If you can make an effort to be involved in campus or community projects, it sends a message about the kind of person that you are. It enables you to help others, to meet people, to develop your skills, and to enhance your marketability. Employers, as we have said earlier, like to know that you have a successful history. Contributing to the community is a good way to help build that history.

4. What is an internship? An internship is a work experience at a placement site appropriate to your career interests. Internships can help you find out what you like (or dislike!), and you may learn a set of skills or how to apply knowledge. It signals an employer that you have experience and initiative. You may always volunteer or be employed at a place of interest as suggested above, but at many universities and colleges, an official internship can earn you credit toward your degree.

Why should I bother with an internship? Internships offer many benefits. For example, they enable you to gain relevant work experience before you graduate, they provide you with employers who are often willing to give you strong recommendations, and they enable you to think through your career options and learn about the ambience of a work environment. Sometimes internships provide you the chance to work in a new city, state or country; they enable you to gain academic credit for your work, and sometimes pay; and finally, they enhance your marketability.

We know of many employers who will not even consider a recent graduate for employment unless she or he has had an internship while an undergraduate. Below we will cover the definition of internships, their pros and cons and sample worksites.

PROS of internships:
- Gain work experience that is attractive to employers and graduate schools.
- Explore your chosen field of interest and investigate career options.
- Experience hands-on application of classroom knowledge and material.
- Meet new people and establish professional contacts for potential future employment.
- May get to experience working in a new city, state, or country.
- Develop professional skills.
- Learn about important issues within your field of interest.
- May receive financial rewards, and/or stipends.
- Can receive credit toward your degree.
- May receive offer for permanent employment from the internship site.

CONS of internships:
- May not be the type of work you envisioned or may be more work than you expected.
- Takes time and energy.
- May not be paid.
- Graduation date might be delayed if you do the internship for credit and carry an additionally heavy credit load.
- May come at a busy time (e.g., finals week).
- May need to have your own transportation to get to an internship site and/or to transport clients.
- May need to purchase appropriate clothing to work at some sites.

What kinds of sites are available? There is
considerable variety in internship sites. It will, of
course, be easier to establish one if you are at a school
where there is an active internship coordinator (some
are housed within academic units). Most colleges or
universities have a list of pre-established sites and
most will aid you in initiating a new site if you have
someplace you would really like to work. To give you a
sense of the type of responsibilities typically given at
internships, here is a list of our more popular internship
sites:

- Crisis intervention for a telephone hotline
- Education for at-risk youth
- Working with pregnant teens
- Training to help with eating disorders
- Human resource training in personnel issues
- Child care training and experience
- Domestic violence work (with children or adults)
- Juvenile delinquent trackers
- Public defender aides or assistance with probation
  and parole services

Our universities are located in regions of at least
80,000 people. Needless to say, if you go to school in
a smaller town, there are probably fewer internships --
just as there are probably more in a larger city. Think
about pursuing an internship elsewhere as well. There
are exciting national and international internship
possibilities --look into them by asking assistance from
your internship coordinator or checking out any
number of excellent guides to internship experiences!

Anything that you do to help develop a set of
professional skills is important and helpful. Many
students are employed in jobs that allow for
professional training, just as many students volunteer

at interesting sites. It is important to realize that your goals and your supervisor's goals may be different at a job or a volunteer experience than they might be if you were an intern. Internships have the expressed purpose of being focused on your professional development, and, most importantly, are designed to give you structured feedback. You may or may not get that from other experiences. While you may be able to get similar experience at other placements, an internship will be your best bet to secure a position with real professional benefit.

5. Why do I need to take special courses? Aren't those in psychology enough? Psychology courses will be a great foundation upon which to add courses to deepen your knowledge base or skills. These additional courses also signal your specific skills and interests to employers. For example, if you are interested in working with delinquents, you may want to take courses in sociology related to criminology or in political science related to law.

What kind of coursework should I pursue?

Elsewhere we mentioned the banker who likes to recruit psychology majors. He said he could train students in the specific skills needed. However, if you were this employer, would you be more excited by a psychology applicant with no banking or financial experience, or by a psychology applicant with some coursework or professional experience? The stronger applicant would certainly be the one with additional evidence of interest and training in the field. You can enhance your appeal to employers in a variety of fields by using coursework to signal your interest or skills.

Below we have mentioned some career tracks and some potential courses to consider. Obviously your choices and options will vary greatly depending on where you are a student; however, you should keep an eye out for courses that would enhance your employability.

Of course, along with specific courses, minors and/or double majors are another way to signal your interests and expertise. None of these courses, though, should be at the expense of real experience. We've had students who are seniors and have wanted to stay in college longer to pick up a few extra courses in a field that was of interest to them. We do not recommend this strategy. Unless you have been specifically advised by an employer or a graduate school admissions committee to take a course or a set of courses, graduating and getting experience will be a stronger path for you in the long run.

What courses should I take in psychology? In other departments? Most undergraduate psychology degrees provide you with a good all-around background in the discipline of psychology. Therefore, the coursework is appropriate to most jobs and graduate programs. In national surveys, psychology majors indicate that the courses they found most helpful after graduation were abnormal psychology and methodology courses, but your needs will vary based on what field into which you go.

As we discuss the various career tracks below, we will mention specific psychology courses if they are applicable and we will highlight courses from other departments that you may not have thought about.

STOP! Before you merrily sign up for courses, make sure to check the course requirements. Many courses may not be open to non-majors, or may have prerequisites that you have not yet completed.

Human services and counseling-related fields: If you are interested in counseling-related fields, you will want to make sure to take abnormal psychology, behavior modification, personality and/or counseling theory, and a course on addictions. However, you should also consider what other departments have to offer (sociology and social work are two potential places to start if your school has these departments). Consider courses that might build skills (for example, our speech department offers an interviewing class) or enhance your knowledge of specific populations (e.g., the elderly, adolescents, preschoolers, rehab clients). Additionally, being bilingual is a real plus if it can help you service a particular population. Finally, if your school offers a course in medical ethics, consider taking it.

Business-related fields: Business oriented students should take courses (or major/minor) in business. Depending on your interests, you should keep an eye out for courses in marketing, management, sales, and courses applicable to human resources (e.g., courses dealing with insurance, compensation and benefits, and personnel issues).

Psst . . . For a career in sales, if you are interested in a specific product or sets of products (for example, pharmaceuticals) take courses that reflect that content area.

Additionally, if you are interested in business, consider some business "basics" such as accounting and economics. Depending on your school, some of these courses might also count toward your general education requirements.

If your psychology department offers them, consider courses in industrial/organizational psychology, behavior modification, group dynamics, and any course that might serve to enhance your ability to work with people.

Law or corrections-related fields: Students interested in law-related careers should consider sociology or criminal justice classes such as delinquency and/or parole, and political science courses on law and legal processes. Students bound for law school should check the specific requirements of the schools in which they are interested and prepare to take the LSAT, a standardized law school admissions test.

Allied Health Fields (e.g., medicine, physical therapy, occupational therapy, dentistry, and chiropractics): The big issue in preparing for further technical training is making sure you have the proper prerequisites for the program. Most colleges and universities have a person who acts as an advisor for students with these interests. You may also need to prepare to take an admissions test specific to your field (e.g., the MCAT for medical school). Finally, don't be afraid of your psychology degree "looking bad"--it may be the thing that makes your application stand out (as long as you have the grades and the prerequisites to go with it).

Psst . . . Students interested in graduate school in psychology-related fields should look into specific course recommendations or requirements that programs may have and should be particularly careful to take advanced research design and statistics courses as well as courses specific to their interests (e.g., developmental psychology).

Overall, the purpose of coursework in your area of interest is to enhance your knowledge of the field. You will also make contacts with instructors and students who may further aid your career development. Remember that although course content is important, it pales when compared to real skills such as good writing, good verbal communication, problem- solving and technology mastery.

Now, let's turn to other issues to consider.

What if I have special considerations? Many students have attributes, which, in various employment situations, can potentially be beneficial or problematic. Common situations include being an ethnic minority in a largely Caucasian workplace, having a physical or learning disability, or being a lesbian/gay/ bisexual person. Often these attributes can work to your benefit if you "market" them to sensitive employers. Other times, you may face overt or subtle discrimination, sometimes without even knowing it, such as not getting an interview. It may surprise you to learn that there are good resources for individuals with special considerations, and we have discussed several of them in the job search chapter (e.g., lists of employers particularly open to hiring ethnic minorities or lesbian/gay/bisexual applicants). If and how you will have to deal with these issues depends largely on your circumstance and your preference. If you have a visible disability or are an ethnic minority of color, you may have to confront the issue. If, on the other hand, you have a less visible disability (e.g., a learning disability) or are a member of a less visible minority (e.g., lesbian), you will have more discretion in dealing with the potential issues. We want you to know that there are good resources available and that you should not be afraid to access them. Your college or university should have individuals who have designated themselves as advocates for particular groups. If not, ask a trusted instructor to help you locate "safe" individuals and resources. If you don't feel you can trust anyone, consider consulting outside resources such as community or national groups.

Psst . . . You should also be aware that that there are on-line employment resources for people of color (e.g., www.imdiversity.com), persons with disabilities (e.g., www.disability.gov, and for the GLBT community (e.g., www.gfn.com).

What else should I consider? Some additional and important points that can help you increase your chances of finding work that is satisfying to you include the following:

1. **Build your communication skills.** Employers rank oral communication and interpersonal skills as very important in the people that they hire. Being able to talk with people and to get along with them not only helps in a work setting, but in most everything that you do. Seek feedback from others about how to develop these skills. And remember that gaining these skills is not a "spectator sport." You will need practice.
2. **Participate in extracurricular activities.** Being involved in extracurricular activities such as professional organizations, student government,

athletics, or clubs signals to an employer that you are a well-rounded person. These activities might also provide specific skills gained through organizing events or working with people who have special needs. As with many of your experiences, one of the key things is how well you are able to talk about and convey the implications of your experiences.

3. **Try an international experience.** Most colleges and universities provide opportunities to study abroad. Take advantage of them! This is probably one of the easiest times in your life to travel without too much responsibility and fares and exchanges are usually kept low. Finally, employers like to see international experiences on resumes.

4. **Keep an open mind about your possibilities.** One way to enhance your career opportunities is to be flexible about the kinds of work you may see as acceptable or "psychological." Also, keep an open mind regarding your geographic destination. Remember that larger urban areas will offer more numerous and more varied opportunities than might be found in smaller communities.

5. **Develop an attitude.** A positive one. Survey after survey indicate that employers look for and reward positive attitudes. Employers are especially interested in your enthusiasm toward their organization and the work they offer. They prefer a "what can I do for you?" message to a "what can you do for me?" message. Along those lines, employers hire people who are actively engaged in looking for work rather than those who are waiting for something to "come to them."

6. **Be savvy about your job search.** You greatly enhance your chances of finding a terrific job by

conducting a terrific job search. For more information on how to do this see Chapter 9.
7. **Don't obsess over your GPA.** Very few employers will care about your GPA if they see that you have the right attitude and skills for the job.

Overall, after reading this chapter, you should feel confident, as a psychology major, that you will be able to get a job. More importantly, you should feel ready to start planning strategies to make yourself more marketable so that you can end up in the career you really want. Keep in mind that each experience that you have becomes a part of your total marketability. Don't wait until your senior year to try to understand how it all fits together but rather reflect on your experiences and skills throughout your college career.

6

Will I make any money?

Yes, but the answer is not a uniform yes--you will make money but whether or not you make a LOT of money depends upon several factors, such as the type of work you do. For example, psychology graduates who work in human services occupations are often underpaid (when compared to other college graduates), and they work long hours. They can be rewarded in many other ways, such as in the satisfaction they gain from helping people, and that is often why they stay with that work, but they don't get rich.

On the other hand, there are many psychology majors who make a lot of money. In fact, a couple of years ago one of our graduates stopped in to say he was just offered a job for $60,000 with a promise of a six-figure salary in the near future if all worked out as the employer planned. By any measure, that is not a bad salary for someone who graduated less than eight months before the job offer. But you need to know that this job offer was in sales, not in a traditional psychology-related field. (By the way, he is still with the company, enjoying the work, and got to attend a training session in France.)

Our point is that you, as a psychology graduate, will have the potential of earning a lot, but it is not a guarantee. Instead, your income is determined in a significant way by the choices you make and by the actions you take to enhance your marketability (discussed in Chapter 5).

If you want to have a hand in shaping your earnings potential, then think about how important a good income is to you. How does it weigh against other factors such as assisting others in a human services work setting, living close to relatives, not having to travel frequently, or not having to meet quotas or deadlines? These factors are not necessarily mutually exclusive with earning a high income, but they sometimes are. Often, people who earn a lot of money are in business settings, living in larger urban settings, traveling frequently, and working with tight deadlines. So these are some issues to consider. But if you want to earn as much as possible and still do what you enjoy, we will discuss how you can try to make that happen. That is a reasonable goal.

What do I need to know about my income potential as a psychology major? First, you <u>can</u> have an impact upon what you earn. When you enhance your marketability, you enhance your chances of earning more. This means participating in internship experiences, obtaining a grade point average of 3.0 or higher, receiving strong recommendations from your faculty and others who can speak to your ability, and taking coursework that supports your career interests. Employers tend to "bid higher" for people who appear to have a potential to contribute to their organizations.

Psst . . . It also helps to know what average starting salaries are (see below) when you are negotiating your salary with an employer.

What type of starting salary can I expect? This depends upon what you are thinking you would like to do with your psychology background. The average starting salary for all bachelor's level college graduates is in the low to mid 30s; however, that includes figures from lucrative careers such as information technology jobs. Some specific examples from different fields are as follows:

❖ **Human Services:** The starting salaries are in the low 20's. To increase your income in this field, you would most likely have to move into a supervisory role or return to school for a graduate degree that would enable you to become certified as a social worker or counselor.

❖ **Management:** The starting salaries are in the low 30s. You would usually start as a manager trainee and after 6-12 months be promoted into a management role. A manager works in many settings including, but not limited to, retail, banking, and manufacturing. Note: the setting has a role in determining the salary.

❖ **Sales:** The starting salaries are in the low 30s, but this can vary widely based upon the type of product being sold. Some sales positions pay on a commission basis only, which means that income is solely dependent on sales.

❖ **Student affairs:** The starting salaries are in the mid 20s, but this can vary based upon the type and size of college in which you   are working, job responsibilities, and whether or not you have a master's degree.

❖ **Corrections/probation/parole/law   enforcement:** The starting salaries are in the high 20s in law enforcement, but this can change based upon the state in which you are employed and the functions performed.

❖ **Customer service:** The starting salaries are in the mid 20s, but these can vary according to the type of organization for which you work.

❖ **Child and youth care:** Starting salaries for child care worker, teacher's aide, and other related work are low. For instance, the median income for preschool teachers is ~$19,270.

❖ **Human resources:** There is an increasing number of entry level positions in this field that starts employees at the low 30s.

For more specific starting salaries and starting salaries in other fields, we suggest you consult the Bureau of Labor Statistics' Occupational Outlook Handbook website at www.bls.gov/oco, or the *Salary Survey*, a quarterly publication from the National Association of Colleges and Employers. It should be available in the career services office on your campus. Finally, there are several good websites for salary information that include concerns such as geographic region and "buying power."

- *www.salary.com*
- *www.salaryexpert.com*
- *www.wageweb.com*

What are starting salaries with a master's degree or a doctorate in psychology? Of course, these figures vary according to the type of work that you do, but APA salary surveys (on 2001 and 2002 data) provide the salaries of individuals in their first five years of work by type of degree. The median income for master's level careers was $34,000. The median income for PhDs and PsyDs in human services was $35,000, as professors it was $37,000 and as researchers it was $ 42,000. However, it is important to note that advanced degrees may indicate more earning power over the lifetime. The median income of all master's degree respondents was $55,000 and for doctorate level respondents it was $72,000.

What if I am offered a salary that is less than what I believe I deserve? If you are interested in the position, then by all means negotiate with the employer. Explain your interest, but also your expectations and why. In other words, you can say that you expect a certain amount based upon the average starting salaries in the field as well as upon your experience and ability. Note, however, that you have to also be realistic about your salary expectations. If you are in a poor rural area, your chances of negotiating for a higher salary may not be as good as in a wealthier urban area. In other words, it is important to consider the context as you handle this issue.

It is also important to remember that certain parts of the country have higher costs of living than other parts. That job in the city might pay more, but it will also cost you more to live there. Before you accept an offer, ask about the costs of housing, food, insurance, transportation and clothing. You want to be certain that you are making a livable wage.

If I start at a very low salary, will that affect my earnings potential the rest of my life? Not necessarily, unless you remain in the same job and never get merit pay or promotions. But while you are in a low-paying job, it is important to continue to grow and learn so that you will have improved skills to offer the next employer. However, it is always best to get the highest starting salary available at for the job offered to you.

Psst . . . Research suggests that far too few women even attempt to negotiate salary. In fact, women are less likely to ask for raises, promotions and better job opportunities too. Over the lifetime of a career this reticence to ask may lead to missed income and missed opportunity. To risk being simplistic, the key to asking is asking. That is, individuals who try to negotiate usually walk away with some increased opportunities or income. At the end of this chapter, we provide two good references. For both the men and women reading this book, it is well worth your time to think about your own feelings regarding negotiating (it's not nice?) and learn some practical strategies. We think this is particularly hard to negotiate for income in jobs in the area of human services. The agency is likely to be financially strapped; however, this does not mean that you should be paid less than a person with the same job just because he "asked" and you did not. Also, as indicated below, salary is not the only thing an employee can negotiate. Think about fringe benefits and/or job costs such as mileage or cell phone reimbursements.

What else do I need to be thinking about? A salary should only be a part of the compensation that you receive for your work. You should also be concerned about the fringe benefits such as the health insurance, life insurance, and retirement benefits that a position offers. Many of us underestimate how much benefits are worth. In general, fringe benefits are worth at least 25-30% of your income. If you do not get these through your work, then you will have to pay for these out of your pocket. If you have a family or a partner, then it is important to inquire about benefits for them as well. Some organizations are now offering domestic partner benefits for gay and lesbian couples. If this is relevant to you, we encourage you to investigate whether this is a part of the benefit package. If you have children or hope to have children, you might also want to inquire about in-house childcare facilities.

What should I do if I like the field but don't like the salary? One obvious answer is to consider graduate study, which usually ensures a higher level entry point into a professional career and thus a higher salary. (See Chapter 7 for a discussion of the financial issues related to graduate study.) Another answer is to consider a career that uses your psychological interests but in a business setting, such as management.

Overall, this chapter has highlighted the types of salaries that psychology majors might expect to make, and canvasses some of the other income-related issues involved in choosing a career. There is considerable variation within and across fields, and it is well worth your time to look into ways to maximize your earnings.

Great Resource!

A good practical book:

Chapman, J. (2006). *Negotiating your salary: How to make $1,000 a minute* (5th ed.). Berkeley, CA: Ten Speed Press.

A more academic and in-depth look at the issues around gender and negotiation.

Babcock, L. & Laschever, S. (2003). *Women don't ask : negotiation and the gender divide.* Princeton, N.J.: Princeton University Press.

7

Should I go to graduate school?

Going to graduate school takes a lot of time, energy, and money. It also requires aptitude and commitment. Often, psychology students think they have to go to graduate school because they mistakenly believe that there are no jobs for psych majors. If you fall into this latter category, re-read Chapter 3 on jobs with a psychology degree. You should only go to graduate school if you genuinely know that an advanced degree will be necessary for your intended career. It wastes your time and the graduate school officials' time if you apply on a whim. It is our opinion that you should be crystal clear about why you want <u>that</u> specific degree and what you intend to do with it after you obtain it. The next chapter in this book (Chapter 8) deals with the nitty gritty of applying to graduate school in psychology-related fields. This current chapter involves a series of questions aimed at helping you discern what issues are at hand.

What are the key issues to consider? Currently, every year about 10,000 students graduate with master's degrees in psychology and another 3,000 with doctorates. Not all of these students started as psychology undergraduates, but when you consider that approximate 75,000 students graduate every year with psychology degrees, clearly not <u>everyone</u> is going to graduate school. It is just not possible or right for most students. Is it right for you? The key issues to consider are 1) What are the general changes of getting in? 2) Are you suitable for graduate school? 3) Do you want/need to go to graduate school? 4) What kind of graduate school do you want to attend?

What are the odds for admission? It is important to know the general "state of the union" when it comes to your chances of acceptance. Under no circumstance do we want to frighten you off, but we want you to be aware that graduate school is very competitive and you will need to make yourself an attractive candidate. Landrum (2004) culled the APA Graduate School in Psychology volume and analyzed applicant and acceptance data in a way that is very helpful to current undergraduates. We have provided a summary of his findings below, but the bottom line is that graduate school in psychology is very competitive, that counseling/clinical areas remain the most popular, and it is still more difficult to get into a doctorate program in clinical psychology than it is to get into medical school. The overall acceptance rate across all specialty areas for PhDs was 15.8%, for PsyDs was 38.7% and for master's it was 53.4%. You can use this information wisely to think about your own plans and the attractiveness of your application.

Table 7.1 Selected data on acceptance rates by type of degree and specialty (Landrum, 2004).

Type of Degree → Specialty ↓ (six most popular areas)	PhD	PsyD	MA/MS
Clinical	10.5%	40.8%	49.4%
Counseling	14.7%		60.7%
I/0	15.2%		45.1%
Social	18.0%		37.8%
School	28.6%	31.0%	46.5%

Am I an attractive applicant? Graduate schools are looking for strong students with the initiative and ability to do graduate work. In particular, they need to know that you know why you want that particular degree. Internship and/or research experience is valued because it signals a graduate school that you have a clue about your future endeavors. Strong grades and strong evaluations also play a major role. You need to show that you can work independently. You must also have the financial ability to pay for the application process and to secure payment (loans, aid, etc.) for the graduate school itself. Finally, you must be a good fit with the particular program in which you are interested.

Psst . . . This may sound harsh, but going to grad school is not just an issue of desire. You must be an attractive applicant. All graduate schools have an admissions process of some sort, and you will have to qualify. We state this here because we often hear students say "I'll just go to graduate school, if I can't get a job." It is not that easy, and it is not a second choice or a default option. Successful graduate school applicants start their planning early and build a set of experiences and outcomes that display their talents. .

Let's take a closer look at several dimensions that you should consider.

Grades. Because many people apply to graduate school, most programs "paper screen" their applicants. They use grades and test scores as quick dividing lines. Therefore, good grades are important. Additionally, good grades show strong study skills that are necessary for graduate school. As a general rule of thumb, any student with a grade point average (GPA) significantly below 3.00 in the major should seriously reconsider graduate school. Once one is above that line there are other issues to consider. First, schools vary in how much importance they place on grades so you may be applying to a school that will weigh other factors, such as experience, more heavily. Second, the better the school, the stricter the criteria will be. Third, most programs have a minimum GPA required; however, that does not mean that if you meet that minimum you will be accepted. Most of the actual GPAs are considerably higher.

In one large national study of psychology graduate programs, the median overall GPA required for doctoral level programs was a median of 3.00, whereas the actual median GPA of the entering class was 3.56. The psychology coursework GPA minimum required median was 3.00, whereas, the actual median was 3.70. For master's programs, the minimum overall

GPA required was 3.00, whereas, the actual GPA median was 3.40. These statistics and many of the others in this chapter come from an article by Norcross, Kohout, and Wicherski (2006b), the complete citation to the article is included at the back of this book in the sources section.

If your grades are not stellar, you will need to figure that into your graduate school interest and your chances of being accepted. In general, master's programs have slightly lower admission standards, and that is one route to consider (see discussion of the distinctions between master's vs. doctorate-level training later in this chapter). As you can see from the data quoted above, the median overall GPA for master's programs was 3.40, whereas it was 3.56 for doctoral level programs. If you are about to eat seven boxes of cookies because your GPA is 3.4, remind yourself that a median number implies that 50% of the accepted applicants were above that number and 50% below.

Both of the books mentioned at the end of this chapter in the "Great Resources!" box have segments dealing with grades (e.g., "What to do if your grades aren't so hot"). Remember that some schools are more flexible about grades. Some weigh other facets more heavily and some will consider improvement in grades. So, if you are like many students and have poor grades for your first year or two but then show remarkable improvement, your overall GPA will carry less weight. However, the bottom line is that if your grades are not great you MUST offset them with other strong selling points.

Standardized tests such as the GRE. The Graduate Record Examination (GRE) that is required by many schools is often also used as a paper screen. Most schools establish minimum scores for their applicants. For instance, in that same national study, the median required GRE total (verbal + quantitative) was 1,050 for doctorate level and 1,000 for master's level programs. The actual median GREs were 1,200 for doctorate and 1,050 for master's. In general, good GREs can really help you, but mediocre GREs (as long as they are above the minimum) won't destroy you. You should be aware that some schools make strict GRE cut-offs, whereas others will be more flexible.

Some graduate programs require additional standardized tests. Two tests that tend to be required for psychology-related programs are the "Psychology Subject Test" and the "Miller's Analogy Test." The Psychology Subject Test can be taken in conjunction with the GRE (for an additional fee) and is a content test specific to psychology. Miller's Analogy Test (MAT) is a mental ability test that involves the solution of problems stated as analogies. Additional information is available at

www.milleranalogies.com.
Your career services should have a booklet describing each of the tests and will know how to arrange for testing.

Psst . . . If you are interested in graduate training other than psychology-related, you will probably have to take the test appropriate to that area. Some common examples are the LSAT for law school, the MCAT for medical school, and the GMAT for graduate work in business.

Other academic strengths. The other criteria that pull a lot of weight in admissions decisions are less objective than grades and GRE scores. In surveys five major criteria are consistently cited: research experience (for clinical and counseling programs also!), professional experience, strong letters of recommendation, strong application essays, and (if part of the process) strong showing in the interview. In Chapter 8 we discuss ways to maximize your strengths in these areas.

Interest and initiative. After you consider your chances of attending graduate school, you still have the more important question of do you want to go. Again, you must really take the time to ask yourself why it might or might not be a good option. "Because I want to be called Dr." is an OK reason, but it probably won't sustain you through several years of graduate work. "Because I can't get a job with a BA" is also a potentially erroneous reason. "Because I want to teach at a university level," "Because I want to be a researcher," "Because I want to be licensed to be a practitioner," "Because I want to a be a guidance counselor, a school psychologist, an I/0 psychologist..." are all good reasons as long as for each statement you can answer the "Why" questions. "Why is an advanced degree needed for this quest?" "Why is this quest important to me?"

As part of deciding whether or not you have the initiative and drive for graduate school, you need to consider that most master's programs take two years (some with summers included), and you should plan on at least 5-7 years for a doctorate. (The median time through is actually much longer, but many doctorate level students start working before they complete their degrees.) Remember, these numbers are the amount of years post bachelor's degree. It is a long haul to get a specialized degree. Many find it invigorating, but many others do not. Only you know if you are interested and passionate enough about obtaining the degree to pursue it. We both have watched brilliant students fail to succeed in graduate school. It is as much an issue of perspiration as it is inspiration or aptitude! Furthermore, you must show a high level of interest and initiative as an <u>undergraduate</u> in order to learn to work independently and show your faculty that you have the necessary drive to succeed in graduate school.

Finally, one of the key reasons that you need interest and initiative is that graduate school is <u>not</u> like undergraduate school. Most graduate students find graduate level work to be more demanding in terms of expectation and amount of work. The course work is more focused, the reading and writing loads are much heavier, and in the later years (especially in a doctoral program) you will be expected to do original, creative, and high quality work on your own. Graduate school is not just "more years of college."

On the positive side, one of the things our students have liked about graduate school is that most of their courses are directly on topics of interest to them--so they find it easier to stay motivated to sustain the high level of work expected.

Finances. Graduate school involves financial investment in two ways. First, there is money involved in the application process. Second, and much more substantial, there is the expense of attending graduate school.

<u>Application costs</u>. Most schools require an application fee that helps finance the large amount of secretarial work involved in the process. The average application fee for master's programs is ~$25 (each). And, the average fee for doctorate programs is ~$30. Some schools charge nothing and some charge over $50. In

addition, you will have the costs of photocopying and postage for the applications.

Psst... Many schools allow for on-line application submissions now.

Plus, there are fees involved in all of the standardized tests (e.g., the GRE) and fees involved for mailing your scores to the various schools. Preparation courses for these tests are particularly costly. Finally, if you visit the schools for interviews or to meet with faculty and see the campus (which we recommend), you will most likely be paying for your transportation and possibly your lodging. At the very least, you should plan on having several hundred dollars invested in the application process alone.

Tuition costs and financial assistance. Graduate students pay tuition just like undergraduates do. In fact, at most universities, tuition is higher for graduate students than for undergraduates. Nationally, tuition rates for undergraduates and graduate students have been rising, and experts do not expect the trend to slow down. Undergraduates at 4-year state universities pay an average of ~$10,000 per year, graduate school tuitions at public institutions average ~$13,000 per year. Fortunately, most graduate students do receive some form of assistance. The most common forms are teaching assistantships, research assistantships, and fellowships. Assistantships require that the student work for the money, and the average workload is around 15 hours a week. Over 80% of departments offer some sort of aid. Traditionally, master's programs offer less aid to fewer students than do doctoral programs.

Recent data suggest that compared to other science fields, psychology doctorate students are more likely to be in debt upon graduation. For instance, whereas approximately a third of the recent graduates had no debt, ~20% had a debt of $70,000 or more! Debt appears to be higher as a result of clinically related programs.

The bottom line is that going to graduate school costs money. In addition to the fact that you are paying money out, you are usually not in the work force so are losing promotion opportunities. While there is no doubt that the starting salaries and the earning potential of students with advanced degrees is higher than those with bachelor's degrees, it is not a given that graduate school is a good financial investment. Additionally, many students graduate with advanced degrees and then have to start paying off both their undergraduate and graduate loans. Also keep in mind that the type of graduate training makes a difference; for example, practitioners make more than academics, and, in the counseling field, those with doctorates make more than those with master's. So, we return to our original point--graduate school is most appropriate to a student who wants/needs the specific training offered; however, it is not always a solid financial decision.

What kind of graduate schools are there to consider? Or master's vs. PhD vs. PsyD, what gives? We are going to give a *very* brief overview of these distinctions here. However, you must become very familiar with them. Each of the resources listed in the "Great Resources!" box at the end of this chapter has a thorough discussion of the issues. In general, master's programs are two-year post baccalaureate programs (often including summers). In most psychology-related fields, there is very little practical difference between a Master's of Arts (MA) or a Master's of Science (MS). Masters programs will aid you best if they are a very specific training (e.g., school psychology, I/O psychology, rehabilitation counseling, guidance counseling, etc.). As we have previously suggested, besides taking less time they also tend to have slightly lower admission standards and less expensive tuition. Many master's programs provide excellent training and should not be considered automatically "lesser" than doctorate programs. The big difference lies in what you want or need the degree to do for you. If you wish to teach at a university level or be an independent practitioner, you will need a more advanced degree.

In general, PhD programs are for students interested in doing research and/or teaching at the university level (currently, 50% of research psychologists work at universities or colleges) and/or for students interested in being licensed as clinical or counseling psychologists. PhDs are offered in the many subspecialties of psychology (e.g., cognitive developmental, educational, experimental, industrial/organizational, social & personality, school, and more "biological" programs like neuro-psychology, and the popular clinical and counseling programs). Doctorates in education (EdDs) are also an option in many fields such as educational psychology or school psychology. EdD programs can differ from PhD programs in terms of coursework and writing requirements, and tend to be available in the more applied fields within psychology. Most doctorate programs take several years, are heavily research oriented, have strict admissions criteria, and are costly.

Counseling and clinical programs together account for over half of the psychology doctorates and tend to generate an extraordinary amount of undergraduate interest. There are several routes available for students who are interested in being clinicians (therapists). They can obtain:

❖ a Master's of Social Work (MSW) degree with a focus on counseling or psychiatric social work.

Psst... MSW programs are not listed in material put out by the APA because social work programs are not accredited by APA. We recommend the National Association of Social Workers (NASW) as your source for information (*www.naswdc.org*)

❖ a PhD in counseling psychology.

❖ a PhD in clinical psychology.

❖ a PsyD in counseling or clinical psychology. A PsyD is an advanced degree for practitioners with much less research emphasis. Although PsyD degrees tend to be offered at private institutions and professional schools, there are many public programs as well.

❖ an MD with subsequent specialization in psychiatry.

❖ There are also a variety of master's level programs in clinical, counseling, and community psychology which offer counseling training that can lead to licensure. For example, a therapist who has a MFCC after his/her name is someone with a master's or doctorate who has been licensed as a Marriage, Family, and Child Counselor, a process that requires 3000 hours of supervised experience and the passage of a written and oral examination.

It is important to note that there used to be a bigger distinction between counseling and clinical programs. Counseling was seen as training for less clinical populations and clinical was seen as very research oriented. If fact, these fields are extremely similar and both boast some of the most competitive graduate school acceptance rates of any field, much more competitive than medical school by the way! A student interested in this area should examine the specific research and training interest of each school. Whether or not you wish to counsel people, a PhD is a research degree, and you will be expected to have some experience with research and be interested in doing research.

All students interested in counseling-related areas should check on the accreditation of the program and make sure it is a recognized accreditation board. Accreditation is often crucial in securing the supervised training necessary for logging the clinical hours required for licensure. The American Psychological Association accredits doctorate programs but not master's programs. If you are applying to master's programs you will need to check on the credibility of the accreditation board. Furthermore, all practitioner students need to find out what type of licensing preparation they will receive. Licensing is usually a state-level issue, but schools vary in how well they prepare and aid their students to be licensed. As with all graduate schools, be sure to ask each school about the employment rates of their graduates as well as salary data if available. Finally, you should be aware that post-doctoral work (one- to two-year research positions completed after graduate study) is becoming more common and is an expected component of training for many subfields of psychology.

This has been a very brief overview. There is much to know about the different fields and the variation in programs. You will need to call on all of your research skills to really become knowledgeable about the process.

What if I'm still not sure about whether or not I want to go to graduate school? We strongly recommend that you take the time to become sure. There are two primary options for you.

1. You can complete your college degree, taking care to enroll in courses that will look good to graduate schools, and then go into the work force. The key issue here is working in a field that will help answer your question. Many students are "burned out" by school and want some time off. However, working as a clerk or server will not help you define your career options. Try to find a baccalaureate level job directly in your field of interest (e.g., work as a case worker to get a better sense of what social workers do). You may never need to go to graduate school because you will find work that is right for you. Or, you may choose to go to graduate school much later in your life when you'll have new and different reasons to attend.

2. You could stay in college longer to get the kind of experience that will help you decide. Only stay in school if you know of specific experiences or courses that can help you. More school just for "school's sake" will not be particularly impressive to anyone. Stay if you can participate in a faculty member's research. Stay if you can complete your own independent research project. Stay if you can audit or take graduate-level courses that will give you a better sense of the scope and expectations of graduate work.

Will it hurt my chances to take a year or more off (e.g., not go to graduate school right away)? It is OK (maybe even preferable) to gain meaningful and relevant work experience before pursuing graduate training. Many students tell us that people have warned them not to take time off. They cite the "you'll never go back" argument. Although "life" can get in the way of graduate school plans, "life" can also shore up graduate school plans. By being clearer about who you are and what you want, you will be a more successful candidate for jobs or graduate school. But, you must spend the time looking into career options and working in the field, or you will defeat the purpose. So, for many students, taking some time off is a good idea, even if they know they want to go to graduate school. Many people go for further education much later on in their careers when they can clearly see the need for it, want to make a career change, or have the interest and family situation that allows for it. Additionally, you should now be more aware of how time-intensive and expensive applying to graduate schools is. You may have more to show for yourself after graduating (e.g., a senior project or additional experience) and you may have more time to focus on the applications.

If you do decide to take some time off, it will help you to alert your faculty members that you will be asking them for recommendations in the future. Ask them what their preference is for handling it. Finally, it may surprise you to know that many employers help finance graduate school for their employees. One survey found that 4 out of 5 employers offer some form of tuition assistance. In addition, some employers will allow for some paid time to go toward attending additional schooling.

Now what? If you are sure that you are going to be applying to graduate schools in the near future read the next chapter. In the "Great Resources!" box on the next page several good books are listed. All of them are helpful; however, if you are still undecided about whether or not to go to graduate school, we particularly recommend the Keith-Spiegel and Wiederman book as a great place to continue your exploration about whether or not to apply.

Great Resources!

American Psychological Association
(2007). *Getting in: A step-by-step
plan for gaining admission to
graduate school in psychology*
(2nd ed). Washington, D.C.:
Author.
www.apa.org OR 800-374-2721

Keith-Spiegel, P. & Wiederman, M.
W. (2000). *The complete guide
to graduate school admission:
Psychology, counseling and
related fields.* (2nd ed.) Hillsdale,
NJ: Lawrence Erlbaum.
www.erlbaum.com 1-800-9-BOOKS-9

Reyes, J. (2002). *The social work
graduate school applicant's
handbook: The complete guide
to selecting and applying to
MSW programs.* Harrisburg, PA:
White Hat Communication.
www.whitehatcommunications.com

A site discussing options for financing
graduate school
www.justcolleges.com/grad/

8

How do I prepare for graduate school?

There are many strategies you can employ to make yourself an attractive graduate school applicant. Additionally, applying to graduate school is a time-intensive and complex activity. This chapter focuses on ways to maximize your chances of getting into graduate school and then covers a timeline of tasks associated with applying to graduate school. The chapter concludes with sections on questions to ask of the programs in which you are interested and what to do if you don't get in. Before you read this chapter, you really need to read the one before it entitled "Do I want to go to graduate school?" Many of the key issues and admissions criteria are laid out in Chapter 7, whereas this chapter focuses on some of the "nuts and bolts" of the application process. So, from this point forward we are going to assume you are knowledgeable about the basics.

What steps are involved in applying to graduate school? There are five major steps involved in applying to graduate school.

1. Decide whether graduate school in psychology is right for you (see Chapter 7).
2. Define the area of concentration and degree that you will pursue.
3. Research schools and programs and choose a range of places to which you want to apply.
4. Complete the applications to these programs.
5. Attend interviews (if applicable) and make a final decision regarding which program you will attend.

Once you have decided that graduate school appears to be your best bet, you need to get busy! It is a complicated and time consuming process that is made much easier if you have good guidance. There are two superb books on the market that are for psychology students who are considering graduate school. One is called *Getting In* and is put out by the American Psychological Association (APA), the other is called *The Complete Guide To Graduate School Admission: Psychology, Counseling and Related Fields* and is written by Patricia Keith-Spiegel and Michael Wiederman. Full citations and ordering information are provided in the "Great Resources!" box at the end of this chapter and the previous chapter. Both books have different weaknesses and strengths. We strongly recommend that you purchase at least one of them, if not both. In the long run it will probably save you money--especially, when you consider the cost of graduate school applications. Keith-Spiegel and Wiederman's is a more thoroughly documented book that answers a wide variety of "special circumstance" questions such as "What to do if your grades aren't so hot?" -- it has also just been released in a new edition. The APA guide is a shorter, more step-by-step guide. Both are around $25 in paperback. Your campus bookstore might carry them too. Because these resources are so thorough, and because these issues need to be discussed thoroughly, in this chapter we will just try to hit the highlights so you'll know what to expect.

When do I do what? Over the next few pages we've sketched out a basic timeline for graduate school preparation. As we have warned, the best time to start is early in your college career. In fact, there is research support for the notion that early planning and its link to graduate school related activities such as research experience benefits applicants. If you are playing "catch-up" to some extent, make sure you are spending your time wisely.

GRADUATE SCHOOL PREPARATION TIMELINE

Your sophomore year:

➢ *Pursue extensive career exploration.*

➢ *Take statistics and research design courses.*

➢ *Volunteer at an organization of interest to you.*

Your junior year:

➢ *Do an internship.*

➢ *Get involved in local psychology clubs. Get involved in national psychology clubs. Become a student affiliate of APA and/or APS.*

➢ *If possible, get involved in faculty research.*

➢ *If you have the option, think about an independent research project.*

➢ *Start to plan and study for the GREs, making sure to take practice tests. You may want to take the GREs during your junior year. Career Services, your department, or your library probably have information and applications. Many places have practice GREs on computer that you can take for a small fee and there are several places on the web where there are free practice GRE questions. You may wish to consider a course, but they tend to be very expensive. You can call the GRE people directly at 1-800-GRE-CALL or visit www.gre.com. Taking the GRE early is a benefit because there is the option of retaking the GRE to potentially improve your score. GREs are now only available in a computer format that has the benefit of giving you a much wider range of exam sites and dates. Additionally, you can choose to see your score or withdraw your responses without seeing your test score.*

➢ *Start investigating graduate programs. Ask your faculty if they know of good programs appropriate to your interests and aptitude. Additionally, your department, your library, and career services all might have resources to help with this. Several companies (e.g., Peterson's) and/or organizations (e.g., US News and World Report) put out annual guides to graduate programs. These resources often provide information such as rankings of programs, program descriptions, and acceptance rates. APA publishes a directory that is a thorough listing of psychology-related programs. Finally, there is come evidence that "where" you go to receive a practitioner doctorate may be less than important than where you go to get a research degree. However, APA accreditation of practitioner doctoral programs is very important.*

Psst . . . *The APA directory of programs is not an easy first step. It provides detailed information about specific programs, but it is too dense for your first swipe through the various offerings. We recommend starting your search elsewhere and then using the APA book to find out more on specific programs that have your attention.*

➢ *Send away for information and applications using the phone numbers and/or addresses found in the resources discussed above. In addition, many of these requests can be made electronically at the school's site.*

➢ *When you request the application packet, make sure to find out the research interests of the faculty in the program in which you are interested. We recommend initiating a literature search on some of the faculty that interest you the most. (PsycINFO is the most efficient way to do this.) Furthermore, we suggest that once you are knowledgeable about their work, you contact them and discuss your interests and career goals. Often, one of these people can serve as an advocate for you in the admissions process if it appears you might be able to work well together.*

Your senior year:

➢ *Visit career services to polish your resume and interviewing skills.*

➢ *Take the GREs in early fall (or before).*

➢ *Double check that you have the applications for all the schools in which you are interested. Organize them by application deadline, keeping in mind that financial aid applications are usually due earlier than the program's deadline. The vast majority of graduate schools have application deadlines between January 15th and March 1st and doctoral programs tend to have earlier deadlines.*

➢ *Secure the funds for the application process.*

➢ *Give your faculty members all your recommendation forms at once (if possible) and give them lots of time (see discussion below).*

➢ *Cast a wide enough web to increase your chances of acceptance. Apply to schools from your "A" list, your "B" list and even your "C" list. Do not apply to a school if you would not go there if accepted. Geographic differences will usually help your application.*

How do I maximize my chance of getting into graduate school? Let's review the central criteria for graduate school admission. In general, we talk about quantitative or objective criterion--primarily grades and GRE scores. However, schools also heavily weigh qualitative information that tells them more about you as a candidate. There are nine key areas of nonobjective criteria that most schools consider. We have listed them in order of ranked importance as indicated by doctoral programs (Norcross, Kohout, & Wicherski, 2006a):

- Letters of recommendation
- Personal statement
- GPA
- Interview (if applicable)
- Research experience
- GRE scores
- Clinically related public service
- Work experience
- Extracurricular activity

We discuss these criteria using the following categories: letters of recommendation, research experience, a composite group we will call "professional experience," personal statements, and interviews.

Before we discuss the criteria, we want to remind you that schools vary widely in their admissions criteria. Particularly important to remember is that admissions criteria to master's programs are usually less rigorous and less extensive than doctoral level programs. Consequently, depending on your record and your goals, master's programs may be a better fit for you. Additionally, having a master's degree will frequently enhance your credentials if you later decide to pursue doctoral level work.

What's the big deal with letters of recommendation? People on admissions' committees know that each of your faculty members went to graduate school and are, therefore, familiar with its challenges and process. Additionally, your faculty might be involved with graduate admissions at your own school. At the very least, your instructors have watched a lot of undergraduates come and go and have a "reference pool" to which they can compare you. In short, your instructors are good judges of your graduate school potential <u>and</u> they should be able to tell the committee why you'd make a good candidate.

Bluntly put, your letters have to be strong. Poor or mediocre letters will hurt you. The only way to get good letters is to do good work and to have your faculty members know who you are. You must, must, must get to know your faculty. Start by speaking up in class. You should also visit your instructor during office hours to stop by and discuss class material or your career aspirations. Don't just stop by to chat. Most faculty are busy people with a lot of students to attend to, and they will want to see a "point" to the discussion. You should ask questions, but also share your concerns and aspirations. Tell them about things that you do outside of the classroom if they are applicable to your aspirations. If possible, try to take more than one class with the same instructor so that he/she will have more to write about. Offer to be involved with the instructor's own scholarship, or have the instructor oversee an independent project.

How do I ask an instructor to write me a letter of recommendation? When it comes time to ask for letters of recommendation, do so with care and forethought. You should arrange a face-to-face meeting with them and ask if they know you well enough to write you a <u>good</u> letter of recommendation. If they say "NO," move on to someone else. They are probably telling the truth! Sometimes you may need to prod them a bit ("I know you don't know me very well, but you know me better than the other faculty members do") but do not push! Again, you do not want a lukewarm letter! You want a faculty member to know you well enough to be able to flesh out the persuasive argument "This student should be accepted to your program" with concrete detail. If you are a student at a large university, you or your instructor may wish to involve TAs in the process. It will be helpful for you to have your TAs get to know you.

If the instructor agrees to write you letters, do everything in your power to make the process painless for her/him. It is a lot of work to craft a good letter, and most of them will be doing it for several students. In the table on the next page, we have the checklist that one of us hands to all students who ask her to write a letter.

Why is research experience so important? Doctoral programs are research programs. They will want to see that you understand the research process and are interested in being a researcher. It is not enough to just find research "fascinating," they will need to see that you have hands-on experience with the tribulations and joys of research. Master's programs too will see research experience as evidence of your interest in and knowledge about the field. All graduate schools will expect you to be critical consumers of research. By the way, it is the research experience that is important; it is less important that the research be directly related to your eventual field of interest. In fact, in a survey with current graduate students asked to identify variables associated for graduate school preparedness, the findings highlighted research participation and quality faculty interactions as two of the most important variables.

IF YOU WANT ME TO WRITE YOU A LETTER OF RECOMMENDATION FOR GRADUATE SCHOOL, YOU MUST:

☐ 1. Discuss it with me face-to-face.

☐ 2. Provide a non-official transcript with the courses you have taken from me highlighted. Add a sheet with any other academic interactions we may have had (e.g., internships, independent study, research, club activities, etc).

☐ 3. Provide a current resume.

☐ 4. Provide a copy of your personal statement that you've written for graduate schools.

☐ 5. Provide all of the forms from the schools (together at the same time, if possible), with typed, addressed and <u>stamped</u> #10 business-sized envelopes. Don't forget to fill in your name on the forms and sign the waiver statement (yes or no). Make sure that I know the names of the schools that will be sending online recommendation links.

☐ 6. Provide a table with the name of each school and the deadline date for the letter.

☐ 7. Get all materials to me well in advance (at least 2 weeks!) of the deadline date (be careful of school breaks when we might not receive the materials).

☐ 8. Whether or not you are accepted, we are interested in what you are doing. Drop one of us a postcard (we will share it). Tell us your plans and your new address. When you are in graduate school, you make a nice contact for our other students.

There are several ways to get research experience. One of the best ways is to ask instructors if you can work on one of their projects. If you work with an instructor you should get good training and an insider's view of the process. Another way to get research experience is to do your own. Many schools have "honors" or "capstone" experiences where students design and carry out their own projects. If not, many instructors will be willing to advise you on a project of your own design. If you do get involved in research, try to present it. There are undergraduate research conferences as well as undergraduate sessions at the regional and national psychological conferences. Experiencing a professional conference is great training for graduate school. You will hear about the newest research, meet other undergraduates and graduate students, and potentially meet faculty from the graduate schools in which you are interested. We also think you will find the whole experience less intimidating than it sounds and will make the world of academia less alien. Both of these things will make the idea of graduate school less abstract. Finally, any student who engages in a research project needs to fully understand its rationale, procedure, results, and implications. It is likely that you will be asked about the research during a graduate school interview.

What about relevant experience? You may have wondered why we have harped on internships so often in this book. Experience is a real plus for the job market and for graduate school. You will be up against older applicants with potentially impressive work experience (especially if you are going into a counseling-related field). The benefit of work experience is that you can use it to help form your career aspirations. Additionally, professional experience may influence the type of training you pursue an/or the research topic you explore once you are in graduate school.

I have "experience"...now what? Just having experience is not always enough. The key is to have developed skills and perspective from these experiences. The real challenge is conveying the meaning of these experiences in statements of intent and/or interviews.

Psst . . . This advice also applies to personal experiences.. If you have a life experience (e.g., you are a recovering alcoholic, a rape survivor, or the child of divorced parents), AND you choose to share this information with the graduate school admissions committee, the key is going to be showing how this experience has enhanced your ability to be a good counselor (or whatever). We would strongly advise not to share personal information that you have not fully worked through on your own first. It is also fine if you choose not to disclose information. Applications are not "bare all" information situations. They are about you adequately presenting yourself, what you have to offer, why you want an advanced degree and why you want it at that specific school.

What about application essays and interviews? Our students find application essays extremely hard to write. They are a sales job about yourself and most of us aren't used to that type of writing. It is crucial that these essays are well written. Have as many people read them as you possibly can. Have the letter read by any professional who is in a good place to judge (e.g., instructors, career services people, supervisors in related work situations). A friend is better than no one, but they probably won't know what to look for.

Psst . . . Do not skip this step! You will be close to the deadline and think "oh, it won't matter, this is pretty good." Don't do it! Ask someone.

Essays serve to let the admissions committee learn about you, your experiences as well as your individual strengths (and weaknesses). Your essay should serve to help them get to know you. From a practical standpoint, the biggest mistake we see in essays is errors. Do not let a single typo or grammatical error go by! The committee will see errors as indicative of your care and ability. The second biggest mistake we see is boring, linear essays (e.g., "I was born in a small town in *[five pages later]*...Thus, I came to the recognition that being a School Psychologist was for me."). While your journey was probably important to you, it is less so to them. Your job is writing a persuasive piece that highlights your strengths and skills and experiences. Try to ground your arguments in a few well-chosen specific examples. Finally, convey your knowledge of their program and how well you'd "fit" with them. Both of the books we've recommended have good sections on writing essays.

Interviews, too, are the committee's way to get to know about you and see if you are right for their program. In many programs you are being trained to work with people, and your interpersonal skills are of utmost importance. Chapter 9, "How do I do a job search?" has tips on successful interviews.

Once I've been accepted to one or more programs, what kinds of issues should I consider? Again, this is just a brief overview, but you should be an active researcher about the program(s) in question. Below we have listed several questions that might help guide your thinking about the various pros and cons of any given program.

- Is there someone with whom you will be "matched" for research interests who will serve as your mentor?
- What are the employment rates for the program? The percentage of their graduates working? In what fields? For what level of pay? If applicable, what is their rate of post-doctoral placement?
- What is the average time to completion of the degree at <u>that</u> program?
- What kind of financial assistance can they provide? Is it guaranteed? What percent of their graduate students are assisted? At what level?
- Ask for the phone numbers of current graduate students and ask them to rate the pros and cons of the program. (You should pay for the calls.)
- For doctoral programs, try to find out about publication rates for their students. What percent leave the program with publications? How many publications do students typically have?
- If at all possible, visit the schools, and arrange to meet with faculty and students and sit in on a class or two. You will be glad you did.

What if I don't get in? Do not despair if you are not accepted into the program to which you aspire. Consider a different degree (e.g., master's vs. PhD), or a less prestigious school, and get more experience. See if some of the schools will tell you why you weren't accepted and work on those areas. If graduate school remains your goal, make sure to continue to enhance your candidacy by pursuing the types of activities we've mentioned throughout this chapter and Chapter 7 (e.g., graduate level coursework, research experience).

Finally, remember that there is decent work without advanced degrees. In fact, we recommend that you pursue an active job search while you are waiting to hear from graduate schools so that if you don't get in, you have some career groundwork laid. Resist the temptation to accept "any" job. Get work in a related field.

Overall, this chapter outlines many of the crucial steps involved in a well-planned out graduate school admissions process. We expect that you've now realized that neither the decision to apply nor the application process is to be taken lightly. If you do choose to apply, we think you will find the time and effort put into the front end will pay off in the long run.

Great Resources!

American Psychological Association
(2007). *Getting in: A step-by-step
plan for gaining admission to
graduate school in psychology*
(2nd ed). Washington, D.C.:
Author.
www.apa.org OR 800-374-2721

Appleby, D. C., & Appleby, K. M.
(2006). Kisses of death in the
graduate school application
process. *Teaching of
Psychology, 33*(6), 19-24.

Keith-Spiegel, P. & Wiederman, M.
W. (2000). *The complete guide to
graduate school admission:
Psychology, counseling and
related fields.* (2nd ed.) Hillsdale,
NJ: Lawrence Erlbaum.
www.erlbaum.com OR 800-9-BOOKS-9

Mayne, T. J., Norcross, J.G. &
Sayette, M. A. (2006). *Insider's
guide to graduate programs in
clinical and counseling
psychology, 2006/2007.* New
York: Guilford.
www.guilford.com - updated every 2 years.

A site on the web that links to college
and university sites
http://www.clas.ufl.edu/au/

9

How do
I do
a job
search?

First of all, when you search for a job or an internship, there is an underlying fact you should always remember and it should guide you as you go through this experience. The fact is that employers want to hire someone who is interested in working for them. Sounds elementary? You would not believe the number of people who only focus on getting a job-- any job--and could care less where they work. Believe us when we say that a job searcher like this does not impress employers. They don't work to hire a "job shopper" but rather a focused employee who knows why they want to work for a particular organization and what they can contribute there. You may ask, how can I know that I really want to work for a particular organization? It's a good question that we will address next. We will also show you how you can put to good use some of your psychological knowledge as you conduct a successful job search.

Psst... The information in this chapter also applies to looking for an internship.

How do I get started in conducting a successful job search as a psychology major? The very first step is for you to decide what kind of work you want to do. (Note that Chapters 3 and 4 discuss the steps to take to decide on job options that make sense for you.) By doing this you will focus your efforts, and you will find it much easier to target the type of employer with whom you want to work.

Another step is to start organizing for your job search early in your college career. Waiting until graduation day not only cuts you out of all the great resources and opportunities available to you while you are a student, but also reduces your ability to be planful about this very important process that is occurring in your life.

How do I target and research possible employers? It's really easier than you think! Often there are directories on the Internet or in hardcopy of employers, such as human service agencies within a given community, that can help you identify leads. If you want information on a specific employer, we suggest you check to see if they have a homepage on the Internet. Or call the organization and ask to talk with someone who has worked there for a while who could give you an overview of its activities and goals. Or go to the archives of your local newspaper and see if there are stories about it. Or check with your career services office to see what information they might have. If none of these strategies work, then brainstorm ideas with a friend or family member regarding ways to learn about the organization. There is always a way to learn about an employer before you apply for a position.

Psst… Review the internet job hunting sites and tips in Chapter 4 of this book.

What else do I need to do to find rewarding employment? You will need a resume that has a positive psychological impact upon the employer, and you will need to be an effective interviewee.

How do I design a resume that has a psychological impact--good or bad--upon anyone? The secret to this is to remember that what you list first on your resume is what is emphasized to the reader. Thus you will want your skills, attributes, experiences, and academic preparation that are most relevant to the work you want to obtain in the most accessible location on your resume. By doing this, you are telling the employer what is most important about your candidacy for them. As they glance through the hundreds of resumes they typically see, yours will stand out because the information they need is up front. Your resume will have focus and that in turn reflects positively upon you.

What else is important about my resume? You will want to show the employer that you have a record of success. Employers believe that your history will predict your future, and so they want to know how well you have done in your past experiences. Specifically, employers want to know what you have gained from the experience or how you have contributed to the success of the organization. If you had an internship, or other kind of field experience, you can highlight what you learned from that. For example, if you assisted five at-risk youths in developing better study habits, your resume could state "skilled at motivating young people."

On the other hand, even if you have not had directly related experience, you can still discuss the skills you gained that could be transferable to another setting. If you have been a bartender you might indicate you developed an ability to listen well to people with troubles and learned when it was appropriate to intervene and when it was not (if you did indeed learn this). If you designed a more efficient way to make Bloody Marys, say so! If you worked in a fast food restaurant, did you learn to think quickly on your feet in a rushed situation? These are all examples of transferable talents or skills that will interest employers. Remember, however, that in an interview you must be able to discuss and explain whatever you put on your resume.

Is there more to know about a resume? It should be error free! Employers are looking for a way to eliminate resumes (because that is an easy way to make a decision) and the quickest way they have found is to toss out those with spelling or grammatical errors or those that are messy, hard to read, or otherwise not presentable. Proofread, proofread, and then have others proofread.

What about my references? References are people who give employers recommendations on you. So you want to make certain they can make positive, enthusiastic comments about you. You will need faculty or your current or past employers who really know you well. Those hiring you are not usually interested in hearing from the family minister, priest or rabbi, nor are they interested in hearing from your Aunt Louise (unless she employed you). To line up your references, you will need to approach each person asking her or him if they feel they know you well enough to give you a <u>good</u> recommendation. If they say yes, you will need to find out how they want to be designated on your resume and what phone numbers (or email addresses) that you should list. Also you will need to give them a copy of your resume, so that when an employer calls, your reference will have the facts readily available to use when talking about your talents.

What categories of information should I use in my resume? Career objective, education, employment, references, special skills, and volunteer activities are all examples of names of categories. You will want to select those categories that most reflect upon your experiences and skills. For example, if you have received honors and awards, then you might want a category of that name. Or if you have given presentations, you might want a category for those (the same is true for publications or international experience and so on). It is very important that the resume reflect your uniqueness!

What else do I need to know about my resume? Many employers say they prefer a one-page resume for new college graduates. However, you can have two pages if your work and other experiences are relevant to the work you desire. Margins, fonts, and format are fun to adjust but the most important thing is a readable, error-free resume that highlights your specific talents. Also, your resume should always be accompanied by a cover letter (often called a letter of application) when it is mailed.

Is a cover letter important? Yes! It is often the first communication that an employer reads from you and so it should make a good impression. By making a good impression, we mean that it should let the employer know why you are interested in working with that particular organization. This means that you must take some time and effort to do the following:

- Send your letter to a specific person rather than to "Sir or Madam" or "To whom it may concern." (If you don't know the name and title, then call the organization to which you are applying to find out.)
- Explain why you are writing and why you are interested in their organization.
- Discuss how you can contribute to their organization.
- Do not explain in your letter how you learned about the opening if you are applying for a specific position. (This information just wastes valuable space.) The only exception would be if you were referred by an employee of the company who is aware his or her name is being used.

I have submitted my resume and cover letter and have not heard anything. What should I do? Give the employer some time. Two weeks is appropriate. And then if you don't hear anything, call and explain that you have applied, that you are reaffirming your interest in their organization, and ask if they have any questions for you. You might then conclude by inquiring about their timetable regarding when they will be interviewing and making their hiring decision.

I have a job interview! How do I prepare? Whether your interview is on campus through the career services office or off campus at the site of the employer, you should prepare in the same way. Remember that employers are interested in enthusiastic people who are eager to contribute to the organization and to learn. How do you convey enthusiasm? It's easier than you think. By now, you should know quite a bit about yourself and what you can contribute. By having this knowledge you can more readily express enthusiasm about yourself. Also, if you have researched the organization with whom you are interviewing, you should be able to communicate specific knowledge of its strengths and why you are interested in being an employee. Finally, you can communicate enthusiasm more readily by being prepared for the type of questions that you may be asked.

Additionally, employers often believe that because you are a psychology major you will be better able to get along with people--in other words, have strong interpersonal skills. If you think that your education has helped you build strong interpersonal skills, then there is nothing wrong in discussing this in your interview. For most employers, an important priority is to hire employees who will get along with others.

What types of questions will I be asked? There is a new twist to the job interview. It is called behavior-based interviewing, and it is used more and more by employers. It calls for different types of questions than have been commonly asked in the past, and we will discuss this new approach as well as the traditional interview approach that many employers still use.

What exactly is behavior-based interviewing? Behavior-based interviewing is predicated upon the assumption that past behavior predicts future behavior.

Thus the employer wants to hear about experiences you have had and how you have handled them. For example, the employer may say to you, "Discuss a time when you had to solve a problem with a group of people. Tell us what happened and the outcome." Now it is important to remember that the employer doesn't want some general statement about how your whole life has involved problem solving with groups. Instead, the employer wants you to recount a <u>specific</u> <u>instance</u> when you had to solve a problem with a group. This could have been during a class project or on your summer job or in dealing with a family crisis. What is important to the employer is that you recount the context, discuss your role in the situation, and then explain the outcome. An example of another question is "Tell us about a time when you assessed someone's need and then provided that person assistance. How did you assess their need and what was the outcome of your aid?"

To answer behavior-based interview questions effectively, you will need to think about and be able to talk about situations in your life that have been good examples of how you have solved problems, worked with others, handled a difficult situation, or used your creative talents. Employers believe that these situations tell a story about how you will perform your job.

Psst... This is true for graduate school interviews too. Additionally, this type of "specific example" is excellent in graduate school application essays.

What is the traditional type of interview? Of course, not all employers are using behavior-based interviewing techniques. Some still use the traditional style, and some use a blend of both. The traditional style interview is usually focused on questions about your perception of yourself (for example, what are your strengths, what are your weaknesses, why are you the best person for the job) and on hypothetical questions (i.e., "If you were working for us, what would you do if a client yelled at you?").

How do I prepare for an interview? The best way to prepare is to think about what an employer would most likely want to know about you and then think about the answers you would give. Even better, role-play the answers you would give with a friend or do it in front of a mirror. If your career services office offers mock interviewing experiences, take advantage of them!

What if an employer asks me a question that seems to be inappropriate? It can happen. We even know of one student who was asked about her sex life! If an employer asks you about your marital plans, your religion, your age, your ethnic background, your plans to have children, your weight or other physical characteristics, then red flags should pop up in your head. Under most circumstances, these questions are not appropriate, and if they are used in making a choice about whether to hire you, then they are illegal. You have three options in terms of how to respond to them:

❖ You can answer the questions as they are asked but if you do so, you should be aware that they could be used to discriminate against you.
❖ You can get up and walk out, saying that you are not comfortable with the questions they are asking and therefore you wish to terminate the interview.
❖ You can try to analyze the motives of the employer and respond to those. For example, the employer may be asking you about marital plans in order to

ensure he or she is hiring an employee who will stay around for a while. You could respond something like this: "You must be asking me this because you are concerned about how committed I will be to your organization. This is to let you know that I hope to be employed by you for many years."

What else should I expect in an interview? You should be aware that interviews might be conducted in many different ways. Sometimes you might be interviewed by a committee, sometimes by just one person, sometimes even over the telephone (often long-distance interviews are conducted on the phone for initial screening). Be flexible about the format, but still be prepared.

What do I do after the interview? Send a thank you note to the employer letting her or him know you appreciated her or his time and consideration.

What else do I need to know about finding a job? There is a difference in strategy in looking for local employment versus employment in another state or region.

Local: Use your career services office, attend career days and job fairs, volunteer at the organization at which you want to work, look at ads in the local paper, use the Job Service or State Employment Service, conduct information interviews to build a network of contacts, identify local organizations using assistance through such agencies as United Way or First Call for Help which usually maintain directories of local human service agencies, use friends and family to put you in touch with possibilities. (See Chapter 4 for other ideas.)

Long distance: Make contact with the career services office in the region in which you wish to locate, subscribe to the Sunday edition (when the most job openings are listed) of the newspaper in the region where you want to locate, use the web, contact any friends in that region to see if they have suggestions or people with whom you can talk, and go there and visit during spring break or during the holidays.

Psst . . . A student came up to one of us at a conference and gave the great tip that spring (especially March and April) is the prime time to look for university-related research positions for students who have or will have their BA/BS. The principal investigators are likely to know about their funding status and their staffing at that time of year and be able to post positions.

International: Investigate whether your college has study abroad sites where on-going relationships are established and where job possibilities might be explored, contact American firms who have subsidiaries in the locations where you wish to go, check with your alumni office to see if any alums from your college are located in the country in which you are interested, and talk with international experts on your campus. Take a standardized language proficiency exam if you speak the language of the country where you are going so your expertise is verifiable.

What happens if I do it all so well that I get several offers and don't know which one to take? If it happens, you can tell the employers you need more time to think through your options, but be aware that many employers are anxious to get a response from you as soon as possible. **Under no circumstances should you accept an offer and then continue to interview. That is considered unethical and it will**

not only damage your reputation but also could damage that of your college as well. When you are trying to decide upon an offer, we suggest you talk to employees who work at the organizations you are considering in order to get additional insights into their work environments and how well they match with your talents.

What if I have a disability? We strongly urge you to become familiar with the provisions of the Americans with Disabilities Act that addresses the extent to which employers need to make accommodations for people with disabilities. In addition, you will want to discuss with a career advisor the information about your disability that you will be required to reveal (or that you will want to reveal) to a prospective employer both on your resume and in your interview.

Is there anything else that I need to know? We have introduced you to some essential elements of the job search--but there is more to learn and other issues to consider, ranging from appropriate dress for interviewing to prospective employee drug testing. So your preparation does not end with this chapter, rather it is the beginning of one of your most important--if not the most important--college projects, to conduct a job search to lead you into a meaningful and rewarding career.

10

I have my job (or internship), now what?

It's scary to start a new job or internship. It makes you wonder why you ever wanted to graduate or do anything different. And, it's especially scary if you get off to a bad start and don't know how to fix it. This chapter is about avoiding bad starts (or fixing them once they happened) and about taking the trial and error out of on-the-job behavior. Yes, we know that sometimes trial and error is the best way to learn, but it can hurt. So, if you would like to avoid some pain and expedite your learning curve, we offer some ideas about how you can start smart in your career (or on your internship).

What should my first objectives be in my new job?
Many new employees--maybe most--think that their first objective on the new job is to demonstrate their knowledge and skills. Wrong. The first objective is to learn about the culture of the organization and about how best to work within that culture. An organization is like a living being which functions best when its parts work well together. And it takes more than blind faith to figure out how those parts work. It takes your conscious effort, but the rewards will be worth it.

How do I learn about the culture of the organization? That seems like an overwhelming task! You start by asking questions and then LISTENING to the answers. And you start with the easy questions, but those you need to know if they are not covered in an orientation. Here is a list of some sample questions:

❖ "What is appropriate attire for work here?"

❖ "What time are we expected to be here?"

❖ "How do people prefer to be addressed?"

❖ "What are the ways that special events are celebrated, such as birthdays and awards or recognitions?"

❖ "How can I learn about the rules and policies of the organization as they relate to my work?"

❖ "What else is important for me to know about the organization and how it functions?"

To whom should I be asking these questions? Obviously the best person is your supervisor, as well as co-workers and support personnel. Make sure to ask more than one person. When you are new it is easy to be taken in by one person's agenda or perception. When you hear the same advice over and over, then you can begin to trust it (such as the boss really gets annoyed when people are late to meetings).

Speaking of my supervisor, what do I need to know about working with him or her? You first of all must remember that your supervisor is usually the person that is the final judge regarding you and whether or not you are an appropriate "fit" within the culture of the organization. Therefore, it is essential that you try to work well with your supervisor. Specifically, you should make the requests and directions of your supervisor top priority. You should seek feedback regarding her or his expectations about you, and then try to meet those expectations. You should anticipate the requests of your supervisor and you must always avoid surprising her or him. And under most circumstances you must not talk about your supervisor, especially in a derogatory way. If, for some reason, you have difficulty with your supervisor, you should first go to him or her and discuss the issue. If that does not work and you have made a good faith effort to resolve the problem, then you may have to approach another person within the organization. But if you do so, remember that you will have to live with the possible consequences of "going around" your boss, which could include termination if not a loss in your credibility.

We have seen very talented and popular people within an organization fired. It was not because they were not doing their job. It was because they did not work well with their supervisor. We are not saying the supervisor is always right. But we are saying that the supervisor usually has the final decision about whether you keep your job or not. To think otherwise is not wise. If you cannot get along with your boss, then you have choices that you should consciously make:

❖ Try to improve the relationship with your supervisor.
❖ If all efforts fail, then talk with appropriate individuals within the organization about the difficulty you have

having, but be willing to live with possible
consequences of doing so.
❖ Find another job.

A special note regarding internships: One of the
benefits of an internship is that you have support. If it
is an internship that is college or university related, you
should have individuals (faculty, career services, or
both) who can help you resolve issues with your
supervisor or your work responsibilities. In particular,
you should speak up if you feel that you are being
asked to do things that are beyond your training or
comfort zone (e.g., leading a group by yourself).
Please tell someone immediately. In psychology-
related fields these kinds of situations have legal and
ethical implications.

**I get along fine with my supervisor. What else
should I be doing?** Get to know people within the
organization. Ask them out to lunch. Find out about
their responsibilities, their projects, and their thoughts
about the organization. Write down their names and
then remember them. Treat them in a way that helps
create a positive work environment, such as sending
them cards when they make an achievement. Let them
know you are concerned when they have difficulties.

**How do I become effective in my specific work
assignments?** A good question and one that can be
answered through six basic steps.

1. The first step is to **get organized** and to keep a
daily calendar or day planner. It's bad business and
can be very embarrassing to miss an important
appointment. Stay on top of your schedule. Anticipate
meetings or appointments that are forthcoming. Spend

time at the end of each day planning for the day ahead.

2. Know your work priorities. And then try to achieve your priorities with excellence and energy. This may mean working extra hours. Remember that you must excel at your current job before you should even BEGIN to think about the next job.

3. Evolve with change. When new ideas come your way, first think about how they might work rather than tearing them apart. In fact, actively seek out new ideas to use for improving your work.

4. **No matter where you work, develop computer skills and then keep updated.** If there is one sure prediction in life, it is the continuing presence of computers. It is a rare work setting where they do not exist. To be effective, you must be able to use them and to develop new skills as the technology evolves.

5. Do all you can to **get along well with others.** As we stated earlier, it appears to us that most people are fired from their work because they were not able to work well with others, not because they lacked the skills to do the job. Seek out the consultation and advice of others, keep people informed, and avoid the easy trap of criticizing the work of others. Instead, focus on how to improve your own work!

Also, remember that getting along does not mean failing to stand up for what you think is important. If you are asked to compromise your values more often than is comfortable for you, then perhaps you might want to think about a new work environment that is more compatible.

6. Avoid the phrase, "That is not in my position description." Instead, if you are given an assignment that is more than you can handle, talk with your boss and negotiate the priority that you should give to your new work assignment as it relates to your other responsibilities.

7. Make sure to tell others when you need help. Some people (often women) end up drowning in their work because they fail to delegate responsibilities to others and because they promise to do more than is humanly possible. If this happens to you, you must talk with your supervisor regarding getting help and about avoiding this problem in the future.

What else helps me in becoming effective in my career? We highly recommend you consider keeping a *work journal* in which you record the events that happened in your work and your analysis of them. We encourage you to especially attend to your role and your effectiveness. In other words, how did you handle the situation, how could you improve, what were you thinking, what were you feeling, and what psychological theory might explain your behavior and others? We have found that a journal such as this can, if maintained over time, give you a great "window" to your work world and enable you to understand your own perspective.

Another strategy for becoming effective is to **seek feedback** about your work from those with whom you work on a daily basis and especially from those whose work styles and personalities are different from your own and from those whom you respect. NOTE: Seek this feedback only if you are prepared to accept it without becoming defensive. When you obtain it, remember that these people have a different approach than you do and thus all that they say may not be appropriate for you; however, the fact that they DO have a different perspective might give you new insights into ways for you to become more effective.

What if I hear through the grapevine that someone has a problem with my work? What should I do? We suggest you make an appointment with that person, tell them you have heard they have concerns about your work, and ask for their feedback. It will be a pleasant surprise for them that someone seeks their advice, and it can be a good learning experience for you.

How do I know if I am "on track" with the direction of my career? First you need to start with your personal definition of success. Does it mean moving up through an organization? Or does it mean providing effective direct service to people in need? Or does it mean providing excellent support to the decision makers? Your definition is what should direct your goals--not the definition of someone else. (You should also make sure your goals are reasonable given your situation--i.e., it could be hard to advance in some organizations if all the managers are young and loyal.)

Once you have thought through what you want your career to become and where you want it to happen, then think about the steps you will need to take to build that career. How do those steps break down into monthly and weekly activities? Examples might be:

❖ What professional journals should you be reading?

❖ What computer skills should you be developing?

❖ What advice should you be seeking?

Answers to questions such as these that relate to your goals should guide your work planning. And should help you monitor how closely you are "on track" with your career.

How do I keep from making my work my life? Your work will be--or should be--an important part of your life, but just a part. There are also other very significant aspects such as social experiences, time for personal business, spiritual needs, and physical needs. Ironically, the better you attend to those needs, the more effective you can be in your career. To do so, you will want to create time for your other interests and pursuits which will involve being willing to set limits and say no at work. Many people experience their first position as incredibly time-intensive. Some of this commitment is a natural "new job" response. However, you should set limits and strive for balance early in your career. They are important skills to develop, especially for those of us who work in emotionally demanding work.

What do I need to know about money? Believe it or not, if you start putting money away now for retirement, even a small amount, you will have the benefit of compounded interest that will reward you for your effort in future years. With student loans due and other new expenses, it is tempting to delay this. Please don't. Even a few dollars a month will start a nest egg for you. We highly recommend reading up on retirement investments early in your career.

What should I do to allow for job change opportunities? You may find that the job or the career you are in is not a good match for you. That happens to lots of people so don't consider yourself odd. To make a change, however, you may find it helpful to talk with a career counselor, to refocus your resume to reflect the new direction in which you want to work, to establish a network of contacts in the field in which you are considering, to take additional coursework, and to join appropriate professional organizations.

What surprises new college graduates the most about their new jobs? College graduates are often surprised by the difference between the culture of college and the culture of the workplace. Holton (1998), researched new graduates perceptions and found several key differences. We've touched on a few below to give you a flavor of how the "cultures" may differ. In college, students receive frequent and concrete feedback. In the workplace, employees tend to receive vague and infrequent feedback. In college, students have more flexible schedules as compared to workers' more controlled schedules. In college, students have some control over their performance levels whereas in the workplace "A" work is expected all the time. Finally, in college there are few changes in the routine, whereas in the workplace there are constant and unexpected changes. We provide these comparisons to remind you that just as you got "used" to college which was strange and different from high school, you will also get "used" to the workplace, especially if you enter it prepared for a different set of expectations.

Could you list another six million things I should be thinking about? Don't panic. We have listed all of these topics to give you a sense of some of the issues with which you will be dealing. You don't need to respond to them all the first day, especially when you are just trying to find out where the bathroom is! However, we encourage you to think about the issues we raised and to revisit this chapter in a few months as your career starts to unfold.

Is it over yet? Yes, this book has come to a close! We hope we have helped with the question of what to do as a psychology major, both now and in the future. We wish you good luck and good skill in your college career and in your professional career adventures!

Great Resources!

Hettich, P. I. & Helkowski, C. (2005). *Connect college to career: A student's guide to work and life transition.* Belmont, CA: Thomson Wadsworth

Whitmore, J. (2005). *Business class: Etiquette essentials for success at work.* New York: St. Martin's.

SOURCES USED IN WRITING THIS BOOK

We felt that APA citation would interrupt the flow of this book, which is meant to be a friendly "first step" for undergraduates. Below, in alphabetical order, is a listing of the many resources that were helpful to us as we wrote this book.

Adams, R. L. & Morin, L. (Eds.) (1995). *The Adams cover letter almanac*. Holbrook, MA: Adams Media.

American Psychological Association (2007). *Getting in: A step-by-step plan for gaining admission to graduate school in psychology* (2nd ed). Washington, D.C.: Author.

American Psychological Association. (2003). *Psychology: Scientific problem solvers: Careers for the twenty-first century*. Washington, DC: Author.

Appleby, D. (1997). *Handbook of psychology*. Reading , MA. Addison, Wesley.

Appleby, D. C., & Appleby, K. M. (2006). Kisses of death in the graduate school application process. *Teaching of Psychology, 33*(6), 19-24.

Ault, R. L. (1993). To waive or not to waive? Students' misconceptions about the confidentiality choice for letters of recommendation. *Teaching of Psychology, 20,* 44-45.

Azar, B. (1996, September). Students need a broader outlook on careers. *APS Monitor,* 35.

Babcock, L. & Laschever, S. (2003). *Women don't ask : negotiation and the gender divide*. Princeton, N.J.: Princeton University Press.

Barry, D. (1983, July 24). Bad Habits. *Miami Herald,* p. 9.

Bloom, L. J., & Bell, P. A. (1979). Making it in graduate school: Some reflections about the superstars. *Teaching of Psychology, 6,* 231-232.

Blumenthal, R. & Despres, J. (1996) *Major decisions: A guide to college majors* (3rd ed.). New Orleans, LA:. Wintergreen Orchard House.

Bolles, R. (2006). *What color is your parachute?: A practical manual for job hunters and career-changers.* Berkeley, CA: Ten Speed Press. (Note – comes out annually).

Borchard, D. C., Bonner, C. & Musich, S. (2002). *Your career planner* (8th ed.). Dubuque, Iowa: Kendal/Hunt.

Borden, V. H. & Rajecki, D. W. (2000). First-year employment outcomes of psychology baccalaureates: Relatedness, preparedness, and prospects. *Teaching of Psychology, 27(3),* 164-168.

Buskist, W. & Mixon, A. (1998). *Allyn and Bacon guide to master's program in psychology.* Boston, MA: Allyn and Bacon.

Buskist, W. & Sherburne, T. R. (1996). *Preparing for graduate study in psychology: 101 questions and answers.* Boston, MA: Allyn and Bacon.

Capaldi, E. D. (2000, February). Universe of the master's. *APS Observer.* 3.

Carducci, B. J., Deeds, W. C., Jones, J. W., Moretti, D. M., Reed, J. G., Saal, F. E., & Wheat, J. E. (1987). Preparing undergraduate psychology students for careers in business. *Teaching of Psychology, 14,* 16-20.

Carney, C. & Wells, C.F. (1999) *Discover the career within you.* (5th ed.) Pacific Grove, CA: Brooks/Cole.

Chapman, J. (2006). *Negotiating your salary: How to make $1,000 a minute* (5th ed.). Berkeley, CA: Ten Speed Press.

Corey, G. & Corey, M. S. (2006). *I never knew I had a choice*: *Explorations in personal growth* (8th ed.). Belmont, CA: Thompson/Brooks/Cole.

Carroll, J., Shmidt, J., & Sorensen, R. (1992). Careers in psychology: What can I do with a bachelor's degree? *Psychological Reports, 7,* 1151-1154.

Ceci, S. J., & Peters, D. (1984). Letters of reference: A naturalistic study of the effects of confidentiality. *American Psychologist, 39,* 29-31.

Clark, J. (199, Fall). Hits and myths about careers in the nonprofit sector. *Journal of Career Planning & Employment,* 43-46.

Clay, R. A. (1996, September). Psychology continues to be a popular degree. *APA Monitor,* 53.

Cronon, W. (1999, Winter). "Only Connect:" The goals of a liberal education. *Liberal Education.* 6-12.

Cronan-Hillix, T., Gensheimer, L. K., Cronan-Hillix, W. A., & Davidson, W. S. (1986). Student's views of mentors in psychology graduate training. *Teaching of Psychology, 13,* 123-127.

DeGalan, J. & Lambert, S. (2006). *Great jobs for psychology majors.* (3rd ed.). Lincolnwood, IL: VGM Career Horizons.

DeLucia, R. (1993, Fall). Breaking into careers in criminal justice. *Journal of Career Planning & Employment,* 29-32.

Dimson, C. (1994). Ethical issues in the treatment of applicants to APA-accredited Ph.D. programs. *Psychological Reports, 74,* 1323-1330.

Everding, M. P. (1997). *Panache that pays.* St. Louis, MO: GME Publishing.

Gardner, J. N. & Van der Veer, G. (Eds.) (1998). *The senior year experience: Facilitating integration, reflection, closure, and transition.* San Francisco, CA: Jossey-Bass.

Gerdes, L. (20006, Sept. 18). The best places to launch a career [Online exclusive]. *Business Week.* Retrieved November 23, 2007, from http://www.businessweek.com/magazine/content/06_38/b4001601.htm

Gilbert, S. D. (1995). *Internships: A directory for career-finders.* New York: Macmillan.

Goldberger, M. L., Maher, B. A. & Flattau, P. E. (Eds.). (1995). *Research-doctorate programs in the United States: Continuity and change.* Washington, DC: National Academy.

Halgin, R. P. (1986). *Advising undergraduates who wish to become clinicians.* Teaching of Psychology, 13, 7-12.

Hayes, N. (1996). The distinctive skills of a psychology graduate. *European Psychologist. 1,* 130-134

Hecker, D.E. (1992, Summer). College graduates: Do we have too many or too few? *Occupational Outlook Quarterly,* 13-23.

Henderson, P.H., Clarke, J.E., & Reynolds, M.A. (1996). *Summary report 1995: Doctoral Recipients from United States universities.* Washington, DC: National Academy Press.

Hettich, P. I. & Helkowski, C. (2005). *Connect college to career: A student's guide to work and life transition.* Belmont, CA: Thomson Wadsworth.

Holton, E. F. III. (1998). Preparing student for life beyond the classroom. In J. N. Gardner & G. Van der Veer (Eds.). *The senior year experience: Facilitating integration, reflection, closure, and transition.* (pp. 95-115). San Francisco, CA: Jossey-Bass.

Huss, M. T., Randall, B. A., Patry, M., Davis, S. T. & Hansen, D.J.. (2002). Factors influencing self-rated preparedness for graduate school: A survey of graduate students. *Teaching of Psychology, 29 (4),* 275-280.

Huss, M. T. (1996). Secrets of standing out from the pile: Getting into graduate school. *Psi Chi Newsletter, 22,* 6-7.

Jalbert, N. L. (1996, Summer). What can I do with a major in psychology? *Psi Chi Newsletter, 22,* 1, 6.

Jannarone, R. J. (1986). Preparing incoming graduate students for statistics. *Teaching of Psychology, 13,* 156-157.

Kahill, S. (1986). Relationship of burnout among professional psychologists to professional expectations and social support. *Psychological Reports, 59,* 1043-1051.

Keith-Spiegel, P. & Wiederman, M. W. (2000*). The complete guide to graduate school admission: Psychology, counseling and related fields* (2nd ed.). Hillsdale, NJ: Lawrence Erlbaum.

Keith-Spiegel, P., Tabachnick, B. G., & Spiegel, G. B. (1994). When demand exceeds supply: Second-order criteria used by graduate school selection committees. *Teaching of Psychology, 21,* 79-81.

Kenkel, M. B., DeLeon, P.H., Albino, J. E. N., & Porter, N. (2003). Challenges to professional psychology education in the 21st Century: A response to Peterson. *American Psychologist, 58 (10),* 801-805

Keyes, B. J., & Hogberg, D. K. (1990). Undergraduate psychology alumni: Gender and cohort differences in course usefulness, post baccalaureate education, and career paths. *Teaching of Psychology, 17,* 101-106.

Kimball, G. (Ed.). (1993). *Everything you need to know to succeed after college.* Chico, CA: Equality Press.

Kressel, N. J. (1990). Job and degree satisfaction among social science graduates. *Teaching of Psychology, 17,* 222-227.

Kohout, J. & Wicherski, M. (2004). *2001 doctorate employment survey.* Washington DC: American Psychological Association.

Kohout, J. (2000, January). A look at recent baccalaureates in psychology. *Monitor on Psychology.* 13.

Kuther, T. L. & Morgan, R. D. (2007). *Careers in Psychology: Opportunities in a changing world* (2nd ed.). Belmont, CA: Thompon/Wadsworth.

Kuther, T. L. (2006). *The psychology major's handbook* (2nd ed.) Belmont, CA: Wadsworth.

Kyle, T. (2000, September). Applications to doctoral psychology program remain steady. *Monitor on Psychology.* 17.

Kyle, T. (2000, July/August). Investigating and choosing: The decision making process among first-year psychology graduate students. *Monitor on Psychology.* 19.

Kyle, T. & Williams, S. (2000, April). *1998-1999 APA survey of undergraduate departments of psychology.* Washington DC: American Psychological Association.

Landrum, R. E. (2004, Spring). New odds for graduate admissions in psychology. *Eye on Psi Chi,* pp. 20-21, 32.

Landrum, R.E., & Davis, S.F. & Landrum, T. (2007). *The psychology major: Career strategies for success* (3rd ed.). Upper Saddle River, NJ: Prentice Hall.

Lawson, T. J., & Fuehrer, A. (1989). The role of social support in moderating the stress that first-year graduate students experience. Education, 110, 186-193.

Leonard, S. (2000, February). Liberal arts majors are 'in'. *HR Magazine.* 184.

Lorig, B.T. (1996, March). Undergraduate research in psychology: Skills to take to work. *Council on Undergraduate Research Quarterly*, 45-149.

Lunnenborg, C. E., & Lunnenborg, P. W. (1991). Who majors in psychology? *Teaching of Psychology, 18,* 144-148.

Lunnenborg, P. W. (1986). Assessing students' career needs at a large state university. *Teaching of Psychology, 13,* 189-192.

Mackenzie, T. A., & Aguinis, H. (1996, Fall). The world wide web: A new resource for psychology students, faculty, and professionals. *Eye on Psi Chi,* 21-23.

Maher, B. A. (1999). Changing trends in doctoral training programs in psychology: A comparative analysis of research-oriented versus professional-applied programs. *Psychological Science, 10,* 475-481.

Mayne, T. J., Norcross, J.G. & Sayette, M. A. (2006). *Insider's guide to graduate programs in clinical and counseling psychology, 2006/2007.* New York: Guilford.

Mayne, T. J., Norcross, J. G., & Sayette, M. A. (1994). Admission requirements, acceptance rates, and financial assistance in clinical psychology programs. *American Psychologist, 49,* 806-811.

McBurney, D. H. (2002). *How to think like a psychologist* (2nd ed.). Upper Saddle River, NJ: Prentice Hall.

McGovern, T. V., & Carr, K. F. (1989). Carving out the niche: A review of alumni surveys on undergraduate psychology majors. *Teaching of Psychology, 16,* 52-57.

McGovern, T. V., & Ellett, S. E. (1980). Bridging the gap: Psychology classroom to the marketplace. *Teaching of Psychology, 7,* 237-238.

McGovern, T. V., & Hawks, B. K. (1986). The varieties of undergraduate experience. *Teaching of Psychology, 13,* 174-181.

McLaughlin, M. C. (1985). Graduate school and families: Issues for academic departments and university mental health professionals. *Journal of College Student Personnel, 6,* 488-491.

Murray, B. (1996, February). Psychology remains top college major. *APA Monitor,* 1, 42.

Murray, B. (1996, September). Students' future is rosier than they think. *APA Monitor*, 52.

Myers, D. G. (2004). *Psychology* (7th Ed.) NY: Worth.

Nemnich, M. B. & Jandt, F. E. (2001). *Cyberspace job search kit: The complete guide to online job seeking and career information* (2001-2002 ed.). Indianapolis, IN: Jist.

Norcross, J. C., Kohout, J. L. & Wicherski, M. (2006a, Winter). Graduate admissions in psychology: I. The application process. *Eye on Psi Chi, 10* (2), pp. 28-29, 42-43.

Norcross, J. C., Kohout, J. L. & Wicherski, M. (2006b, Spring). Graduate admissions in psychology: II. Acceptance rates and financial considerations. *Eye on Psi Chi, 10* (3), pp. 20-21, 32-33.

Norcross, J. C., Nanych, J. M. & Terranova, R. D. (1996). Graduate study in psychology: 1992-1993. *American Psychologist, 51,* 631-643.

O'Hara, S. (2005). *What can you do with a major in psychology?* Hoboken, N.J.: Wiley.

Osberg, T. M., & Raulin, M. L. (1989). Networking as a tool for career advancement among academic psychologists. *Teaching of Psychology, 16,* 26-28.

Peterson, D. R. (2003). Unintended consequences: Venture and misadventure in the education of professional psychologists. *American Psychologist, 58 (10),* 791-800.

Pinkley, R. L. & Northcraft, G. B. (2000). *Get paid what you're worth: The expert negotiator's guide to salary and compensation.* New York: St. Martin's Press.

Poe, R. E. (1988). A decision tree for psychology majors: Supplying questions as well as answers. *Teaching of Psychology, 15,* 210-213.

Poe, R. E. (1990). Psychology careers material: Selected resources. *Teaching of Psychology, 17,* 175-177.

Purdy, J. E., Reinehr, R. C., & Swartz, J. D. (1989). Graduate admissions criteria of leading psychology departments. *American Psychologist, 44,* 703-705.

Rajecki, D. W. & Anderson, S. L. (2004). Career pathway information in introductory psychology textbooks. *Teaching of Psychology, 31(2),* 116-118.

Rapoport, A. I., Kohour, J. & Wicherski, M. (2000). *Psychology doctorate recipients: How much financial debt at graduation?* (Issue Brief 00-321). Washington DC: National Science Foundation.

Scheirer, C. J. (1983). Professional schools: Information for students and advisors. *Teaching of Psychology, 10,* 11-15.

Shaffer, D. R., & Tomarelli, M. (1981). Bias in the ivory tower: An unintended consequence of the Buckley Amendment for graduate admissions? *Journal of Applied Psychology, 66,* 7-11.

Singleton, D., Tate A. C. & Kohout, J. L. (2003). *2002 master's, specialist's, and related degrees employment survey.* Washington DC: American Psychological Association.

Smith, D. (2001, February). The career path less traveled. *Monitor on Psychology,* pp. 21-42.

Smith, R. A. (1985). Advising beginning psychology majors for graduate school. *Teaching of Psychology, 12,* 194-198.

Stanovich, K.E. (2000). *How to think straight about psychology.* (6th Ed.) New York: HarperCollins.

Sternberg, R. J., Dietz-Uhler, B. & Leach, C. (2003). *The psychologist's companion: A guide to scientific writing for students and researchers* (4th ed.). NY: Cambridge University Press.

Sternberg, R. J. (Ed.). (1997). *Career paths in psychology: Where your degree can take you.* Washington, DC: American Psychological Association.

Tsapogas, J. (2004). *Employment outcomes of recent science and engineering graduates vary by field of degree and sector of employment.* (NSF 04316). Arlington, VA: National Science Foundation.

Thomas, J. H. & McDaniel, C. R. (2004). Effectiveness of a required course in career planning for psychology majors. *Teaching of Psychology, 31(1),* 22-26.

Ware, M. E. (1995, May/June). Academic advising for undergraduates. *APS Observer,* pp. 32-33, 36.

Ware, M. E., & Meyer, A. E. (1981). Career versatility of the psychology major: A survey of graduates. *Teaching of Psychology, 8,* 12-15.

Whitmore, J. (2005). *Business class: Etiquette essentials for success at work.* New York: St. Martin's.

Wiley, C. (1992, Winter). Career management for human resource professionals. *Journal of Career Planning & Employment,* 41-45.

Williams, S., Wicherski, M. & Kohout, J. (2000). *Salaries in psychology 1999: Report of the 1999 salary survey.* Washington DC: American Psychological Association.

Woods, P. J., & Wilkinson, C. S. (Eds.). (1987). *Is psychology the major for you? Planning your undergraduate years.* Washington, DC: American Psychological Association.

NOTES

NOTES

NOTES

NOTES

NOTES

NOTES

NOTES